w. GORDON EAST obtained his degree in History at Cambridge University and has been a Lecturer at the London School of Economics. Since 1947 he has been Professor of Geography in the University of London at Birkbeck College. He is also the author of *Man's Environment*.

The Geography behind History

. . . the rills that rise

Sing such a history
Of come and gone,
Their every drop is as wise
As Solomon.

WALTER DE LA MARE, *All That's Past*

If joined together, [History and Geography] crown
our reading with delight and profit ; if parted, [they]
threaten both with a certain shipwreck.

DR HEYLYN, *Cosmographia* (1649)

THE
GEOGRAPHY BEHIND
HISTORY

W. GORDON EAST, M.A.

W · W · NORTON & COMPANY

New York · London

COPYRIGHT © 1965 BY W. GORDON EAST

First published in the Norton Library 1967
by arrangement with Thomas Nelson & Sons Ltd.

W. W. Norton & Company, Inc., 500 Fifth Avenue, New York, N.Y. 10110
W. W. Norton & Company Ltd., 37 Great Russell Street, London WC1B 3NU

PRINTED IN THE UNITED STATES OF AMERICA

8 9 0

ISBN 0-393-00419-8

CONTENTS

LIST OF SKETCH-MAPS AND DIAGRAMS

CHAPTER I

Geography as an Historical Document

And these are things that come not to the view
Of slippered dons who read a codex through.

FLECKER, *Invitation*

EVEN today, if only by its more dramatic interventions, a relentless nature makes us painfully aware of the uneasy terms on which human groups occupy and utilise the surface of the earth. The common boast that man has become master of his world has a hollow ring when we recall the recurrent floods and famines which afflict the peasants of northern China, the devastating floods in the Netherlands in 1933, the more recent destruction by earthquakes of villages in Iran in 1957 and 1960, the assertion that in Central Africa ' the desert is on the move,' the widespread soil erosion in parts of Africa and in the Middle West of the United States, and finally, the continual threat of drought which hangs over the great grain lands of the world—alike in the United States, Canada, and South Russia. These and similar happenings or forebodings serve to emphasise the fact that, even for peoples which have reached high levels of material culture, the physical environment remains a veritable Pandora's box, ever ready to burst open and to scatter its noxious contents. And if it is clear that we cannot today, with all our resources of science, technique, and motive power, evade or control all the dangers and difficulties which are implicit in our habitat, how much more severe and forbidding must these have been in earlier stages of human history, when men were ill equipped to try and adapt the physical stage ! So much so, that in its beginnings, it is often said, history is all geography, for we know that, at a primitive stage of culture and for countless millennia, folk lived on the sufferance of an omnipotent nature which they had little power either to modify or to exploit. In the course of history, however, if they never learnt fully to control nature, many different peoples in different parts of the earth succeeded, by understanding it, in making better and better adjustments to it.

It would be misleading to envisage the geography behind history solely in terms of the dramatic episodes in which it plays continually a leading part. It is not so much by its more violent manifestations—its earthquakes and volcanic eruptions, and its hurricanes and its floods —as by the expression of its normal everyday personality that the physical environment left its mark on human history. If we assume that, however extensive its province, geography includes above all the study of physical environment, our central problem is to discover in what ways and to what extent this environment affected history. For the environmentalists who, following the lead given by certain philosophers of ancient Greece, sought to explain the manifold complexities of historical phenomena in terms of a single factor— geography, this question was easily solved. This geographical determinism, so-called, which found in the differences in geographical endowment from place to place a visible master key to history, has not for some time found authoritative support, and A. J. Toynbee, who restated its case in the course of a general discussion of historical causation, had no difficulty in showing its inadequacy.[1] But if we cannot accept as worthy of credence a complete geographical interpretation of history, what is the proper place to be assigned to geography in the study of history ?

The claim of geography to be heard in the councils of history rests on the firm basis that it alone studies comprehensively and scientifically, by its own methods and technique, the setting of human activity, and further, that the particular characteristics of this setting serve not only to localise but also to influence part at least of the action. The familiar analogy between geography and history as the stage and the drama is in several respects misleading, for whereas a play can be acted on any stage regardless of its particular features, the course of history can never be entirely unaffected by the varieties and changes of its setting. History, again, unlike drama, is not rehearsed before enactment, and so different and so changeful are its manifestations that it certainly lacks all unity of place, time, and action.

In short, in studying the inescapable physical setting to history, the

---

[1] A. J. Toynbee, *A Study of History*, vol. i (1934), pp. 249-71.

geographer studies one of the elements which make up the compound, history : he examines one of the strands from which history is woven. He does not assert foolishly that he can detect, still less explain, all the intricate and confused patterns of the tapestry. He does assert, however, that the physical environment, like the wicket in cricket, owing to its particularities from place to place and from time to time, has some bearing on the course of the game.

Before we discuss more fully the contribution which geography can offer to history, we may pause to inquire what is the nature of history itself. In his ambitious task to unfold and interpret human thought and action as these were ever changing in place and in time, the historian relies essentially on the literary record, incompletely and sporadically though this has survived. But—as he continually enlarged the field of his investigations from the deeds of kings and heroes and from the fortunes of kingdoms and empires to the everyday life of ' the mere uncounted folk '—the historian has been compelled to make use, not without profit, of the collateral work of other social scientists, such as the archaeologist, the anthropologist, and the experts in linguistic and place-name study. Since for certain periods and areas the literary and other historical data are scanty or conflicting, and since, however adequate the record, written history, despite every precaution of care and honesty, must reflect in some measure the personal outlook and interpretation of the historian ; and since, too, every generation should and does write its own history—for these and similar reasons, a critic might suggest that, as Goethe's Faust put it and as Napoleon professed, ' history is the invention of historians.' Some historians, notably A. J. Toynbee, believe, however, that the events of history conform to patterns, or possess an inherent rationality, which exists independently of the historian's mind. On the other hand, H. A. L. Fisher, who was no less entitled to pronounce judgment on this philosophic issue, found in history ' no plot, rhythm or pattern, but only a series of emergencies, the play of the contingent and unforeseen.' In any case, whatever theory of history we may adopt, we must agree that a great deal is now known about the past, especially about the last 6,000 years or so, during which civilised life existed in certain parts of the earth. We need not, following Dr Inge in a cynical mood, agree that ' the things that we know about the past may be divided into those which probably never happened, or those which do not much matter.' Rather we must be impressed by the great mass of ascertained knowledge which has been, and is being continually,

3

accumulated, thanks above all to an intensive monographic research which, by scientific method and great specialisation, historians practise today. And whether he takes for his canvas the problems of a small area during a short period, or whether he is concerned with the problems of ' societies which have greater extension in Space and Time than national states, or city states, or any other political communities ' —what A. J. Toynbee regards as ' the intelligible fields for human study '—it is certain that at many points the historian can enrich and deepen his study by an understanding of the geographical background to his problems. For human thought and action have their springs, not in a spatial vacuum, but in some definite geographical milieu, which defines in varying degrees the character and orbit of human effort.

History and geography, it may be insisted, do not form the sharp antithesis suggested by those who would distinguish them broadly as the studies of Man and the Earth. The idea, not yet wholly dead, that history begins where geography leaves off, on the ground that the latter is concerned exclusively with physical facts, derives from a conception of geography which is no longer current amongst its practitioners. Certainly it cannot be over-emphasised that the central purpose of geography is the study of country—in all its many facets and in all its complex interrelationships—but country almost inevitably includes man, an important agent in its development, and an agent which we, as members of the only surviving human subspecies (*Homo sapiens*), are not prone to ignore. Since every historical event occurs both in space as well as in time, history cannot, except in some of its more specialised branches, be dissociated from country or place. For if ' Geography without History seemeth a carkasse without motion, so History without Geography wandreth as a Vagrant without a certaine habitation.' Since history must concern itself with the location of the events which it investigates, it must continually raise, not only the familiar questions Why ? and Why then ? but also the questions Where ? and Why there ? And it is primarily to the solution of these latter questions that geography can contribute, ' for it has been Nature, rather than Man, hitherto, in almost every scene, that has determined where the action shall lie. Only at a comparatively late phase of action does Man in some measure shift the scenery for himself.' [1] To allocate some of the above questions to separate fields of study, though

[1] J. L. Myres, *Cambridge Ancient History*, 2nd ed. (1928), vol. i, pp. 2–3.

it may be necessary in practice and though it may serve academic convenience, only erects a barrier across a single arena. The close association between history and geography which is enforced in the universities of France and has no parallel in our own, underlines the fact that these studies are continually and logically interrelated. For if history has something to gain from geography, geography, concerned though it is primarily with the present, stands no less in need of the illumination cast by history.

By the layman with small history and less geography, the latter in its modern form is the less understood. In its beginnings one of the intellectual products of Classical Greece, geography made great advances in Germany in the 19th century, and developed rapidly there and elsewhere during the last few decades. It remains, however, in many respects a youthful and growing science, for although the world has been virtually explored, much remains to be done to deepen our understanding of its constituent parts. It may be both useful and relevant to our present inquiry to indicate the present scope and purpose of geography, for, unless we were fortunate, the dimly remembered geography of our school days will avail us little. Just as the physicist is concerned with the study of the atom and its subdivisions, and as the sociologist is concerned with social groups of varying scale and complexity, so the geographer has for his unit of study the region. The efforts of geographers, though diverse and many-sided, converge above all on one common goal—the discovery, description, and demarcation of regions—broadly uniform areas of country which can be distinguished on a scientific basis. But ' regional geography ' has more ambitious aims than this : though it is focused primarily on country in its physical aspect, it seeks continually to detect and to define the interrelationships which exist between human communities and the physical background to their work and movements. And the more important a region becomes to man, and the more complex becomes in consequence the interaction of Place and Folk, the more does it become a significant and intelligible field for geographical study.[1]

The conception of the region forms the main citadel of geography. A region, whether it is large or small, consists of an area of country, not arbitrarily defined as on a sheet of a large-scale map, but distinguished by a certain uniformity in either a physical or a human

[1] For a brief discussion, see S. W. Wooldridge and W. G. East, *The Spirit and Purpose of Geography*, 5th ed., 1958, pp. 140–60.

sense. The geographical elements which are compounded in any area of land, which can be analysed separately but are in fact interdependent, range from climate, position, structure, land forms (including relief and drainage), soils, and vegetation, to human societies themselves and all that they have engraved upon the soil. We must note, too, as another distinct feature of any place, the presence of wild and domesticated animals, of fish and of insects, such as the anopheles mosquito and the tsetse-fly, which have an obvious importance as environmental facts. It is easy to see how very interdependent are these many ingredients of any place. The position of an area in latitude, that is in relation to the sun, broadly determines its climate, though this is governed also by its position in relation to land and sea and also by its elevation and aspect. Climate, too, acting through the natural vegetation, is often the chief determinant of soils, although these may have weathered from local rocks, or have been transported through the agencies of ice, water, or wind. Climate and soils, again, set limits to the range of permissible vegetation, and thus condition the food supplies of man and beast.[1] The geological structure of an area provides one of the chief keys to its land forms and relief features, as it serves also to indicate where, and at what levels, resources of water, coal, petroleum, and metals may be sought.

All these and other interconnected factors condition, though they do not determine, the activities of man, who is himself no mean agent of geographical change. He can, and from early times did, modify drainage, soils, and existing vegetation. If in only a minor degree, he can alter the relief of the land—witness the great tip-heaps of our mining districts. Clever as he is, man must take climate as it comes, although by careful observation he can try and predict the vagaries of weather and modify their effects. By resort to irrigation, where this is possible and profitable, by erecting screens against harmful winds, by using glasshouses, and by plant breeding, he makes use of the climates which he cannot control. He can also, though this marks a modern phase, escape in some measure from the limitations of climate by the practice of substitution : by growing sugar beet where the sugar cane will not grow, and by making synthetic rubber in temperate latitudes. Successful attempts in Arctic Russia to grow green vegetables beneath the frozen subsoil by means of electric light and heat, derived from wind power, show the lengths to which human ingenuity

---

[1] See below, Chapter VIII.

6

can go, although flying in the teeth of climate usually proves an expensive hobby. You could probably grow potatoes even at the North Pole, it has been suggested, if you put a university professor beside each potato to make it grow ! [1]

Since the geographical texture of any tract is made up of so many interwoven strands, how is it possible to distinguish regions which in some important respect form distinct entities ? In fact, this task can be attempted in so many ways that the captious critic might affirm that regions exist only in the minds of geographers. But reflection will suggest that certain kinds of regions, namely those which are styled ' natural ' or ' physical,' possess an objective existence that can be easily demonstrated to whosoever has eyes to see. These physical divisions of the land, even though their boundaries may be zones rather than lines, are differentiated in terms of climate, structure, land forms, or soils, or of some combination of these. Climate suggests the first simple subdivision of the earth's surface into regions where, under broadly uniform climatic conditions, vegetation, whether natural or cultivated, has distinctive characteristics and significant limitations. Soils often provide in continental areas a sharp indication of major changes in the geographical background. Thus, on the Russian platform, which consists of an unyielding crust-block, a deep cover of soils, dissimilar in texture and quality, is disposed along, roughly, east-west zones. So also, in country of varied physique such as our own, a large number of small regions, which often retain a traditional nomenclature, are distinguishable on the basis chiefly of land forms. We may recall, as illustrations, our many vales—the vales of Pickering, Aylesbury, Holmesdale, and Pewsey ; our many downland plateaux, with their abrupt escarpments and their gentle dip-slopes—the Chilterns, the Yorkshire Wolds, the North and South Downs ; our high moorlands —Dartmoor, the Scottish Highlands, and Stainmoor in the Pennines ; our marshlands—the Somerset Levels and the great Fenland ; and finally, a once semi-steppe area, today tree-clad, the Breckland of west Norfolk.

In demarcating physical regions we divide up the present landscape as it has been moulded in the course of a long history, the events of which include the folding and faulting of rocks, erosion, glaciations, subsidences, and elevations. It will be obvious that the detection and demarcation of small regions calls for a special training, alike ' in

[1] See H. P. Smolka, ' The Economic Development of the Soviet Arctic, *The Geographical Journal*, lxxxix (1937), pp. 327–38.

the field' and in the interpretation of geological and topographical maps, but it may be insisted that the fact, if not the detail, of regional differences in the 'physique' or 'build' of the land is self-evident.   Nor from the standpoint of history can the importance of these differences be ignored, for in the main they are of a permanent order, and if they are understood in their present form, this understanding can be applied to the study of the past.

The geographer, then, seeks to discover the patterns which have been etched on the surface of the earth, to find some symmetry in what appears at first sight a confused and disordered scene. When he has found these regions, he attempts to show how far human communities are using the opportunities which they permit—in occupying and settling the land, in exploiting natural resources, in moving to and fro in the course of migration, trade, travel, and war ; and finally, in adapting the region to their needs and in being, in turn, adapted by it. What is the bearing of all this on our inquiry into the geography behind history ?

The answer is that by means of the regional method the geographer has evolved a distinctive mode of thinking which can be applied no less to the past than to the present with which he is mainly preoccupied. His knowledge of the diversity of the earth's surface can be thrown back into the historical past and thus becomes a document, not strictly contemporary it is true, but none the less revealing and relevant to the historian's task. Geography, at least in its physical aspect, provides a common denominator to all historical periods : more ancient than Methuselah, the land has witnessed and survived the advent of man and the ephemeral episodes of his purposive adventure. And, since the many differences in the form of the land—in its climate, its position, and its natural resources—set limits to human effort, these must be the historian's concern. It is not enough, in studying history, merely to consult the atlas map in order to ascertain the position and areas of countries or the location of battlefields and cities. Yet not so long ago the geography contained in sober historical writings was either entirely lacking or assumed this jejune form. Freeman's notable and still useful work, *The Historical Geography of Europe*, for example, included an atlas volume, the numerous maps of which showed no indication whatever of the physical features of this continent. To the uninitiated reader the inference was that the peoples and states of Europe developed on a uniform plane surface ; yet, in fact, no area of comparable size appears so remarkably variegated as Europe, alike in structure, relief, and climate.

At this point the explorer into the borderlands of history and geography should cautiously halt. Can he safely claim stability for the conditions of physical geography, or, to use an alternative phrase, the ' natural landscape ' ? Certainly geographical position in its absolute sense is immutably determined, but in a relative sense, as we shall discuss later,[1] position is a variable during historical times. Again, has climate, which in its direct and indirect effects is usually the most potent and exacting factor in any physical environment, remained constant throughout history ? We shall turn to this problem later,[2] but we may note here that, despite many doubts and much controversy, the hypothesis of climatic change, especially in prehistory, cannot be safely ignored. In contrast, the morphology of the land—that is, its land forms, relief, and drainage features—shows remarkable stability, since its normal changes are effected during much greater periods of time than that of history. Only to a small extent have morphological changes occurred during what is, measured on a geological scale, the minute span of human history. Even so, these small and sporadic physical changes have sometimes had significant human effects. Volcanic eruptions and earthquakes in regions of youthful structure ; subsidence or elevation of the land relative to sea-level ; changes in the courses of rivers and the silting of their estuaries ; the erosion of coastlands and the accretion of new land along coasts through marine or fluvial agencies ; the encroachment of the desert owing to the drift of wind-borne sand ; the loss of soil through erosion, though this may be indirectly due to man's activities : such changes, however insignificant geologically, may have important social results. Further, it should be noted that, particularly in areas which have been long settled or intensively exploited, the natural vegetation which clothed the surface in the remoter prehistoric times has almost entirely disappeared, and even in relatively undeveloped areas, such as the Amazon and Congo Basins, some at least of the primitive vegetation has been removed.[3] So long and so persistent have been man's efforts to adapt certain lands to his use that, in respect of fauna, flora, and even soils, these present a ' humanised ' landscape very different from the natural landscape which confronted their first

---

[1] See below, Chapter III.
[2] See below, Chapter IV.
[3] See below, Chapter VIII, pp. 120–1.

settlers. Egypt provides an excellent illustration of this fact,[1] yet it has been written : [2]

> Egypt is a palimpsest in which the Bible is written over Herodotus, and the Koran over that ; the ancient writing is still legible through all.

And it is reasonable to infer that some of the traditional features of Egyptian life, which appear to this day—in religious ceremonial, in handicrafts, in dress and ornaments, as in the produce of the soil—owe something to the very distinctive physical setting which conditioned Egyptian civilisation.

Whoever would attempt to reconstruct for any past period the geographical setting of any area undertakes, therefore, a task which calls for a certain technique, considerable care, and no less industry. The basic task is to discover the physical properties and potentialities of the area—to discover what economic possibilities existed, what facilities or difficulties it presented for movement within and for contact with the outside world, what natural defences it afforded, and what modes of life it permitted. If, further, he wished to extend his inquiry beyond the physical setting as such, and to try and find what were the human features engraved on the soil at a particular period, the student would have to embark upon a much more difficult task. He would have to discover what kinds of settlements existed and how they were distributed ; what routeways were available ; what mineral resources were being exploited, and where ; how the land was being used ; and how the population was distributed. Such an inquiry falls within the specialist field now generally known as ' historical geography,' for its chief purpose is geographical, namely the reconstruction of past geographies. Yet such an inquiry, if completed in so far as available evidence allowed, would be valuable to the historian no less than to the geographer. It would help to illuminate, on the one hand, economic and social history, and on the other, present-day geography.

Let us now state the upshot of this discussion. Since all human events occur in space as well as in time, the historian, though he is interested primarily in changes in time, cannot neglect the problems of location. Into these problems geography intrudes, for the setting to history limits man's freedom of action differently from place to place,

[1] See below, Chapter IX.
[2] Cited by P. E. Newberry, ' Egypt as a Field for Anthropological Research,' *British Association Report*, 1923 (1924), p. 193.

and thus localises many events. Further, the geography behind history affords at least a partial explanation of the means of livelihood sought by peoples in different areas.[1] Admittedly, ' modes of life ' are not rigidly enforced by physical circumstances. Human groups themselves —according to their stage of cultural development, their needs and their enterprise—determine their means of livelihood, as also their means of transport,[2] yet these are always restricted, sometimes very rigidly, by the nature of the habitat. Again, resort to geographical method sometimes throws unsuspected light on the facts of history. The geographer's practice of making ' distribution maps ' is not only a convenient and precise means of answering the question, Where ? It may also suggest that distributions conform to patterns which can be explained in geographical terms. The established use of this method by archaeologists, who have recognised for some time the importance of the spatial aspect of their discoveries, needs no justification, since it has yielded much fruit. That it can be applied with similar success to historical materials is no less apparent, and becomes increasingly evident. It must not, of course, be inferred that all distributions can be explained in terms of the physical background ; the preparation of a distribution map is rather an experiment, which may or may not come off.

As an illustration we may examine briefly Greek colonisation in the 5th century B.C. If a distribution map of Greek colonies is made (Fig. 1), and if it is studied in relation to other geographical facts and distributions, a number of conclusions can be drawn of historical value. The first and most obvious conclusion is that these colonies were strung out along the shores of the Mediterranean and Black Sea, as Plato put it, ' like ants and frogs around a pool.' It will be noted next that Greek colonies are relatively fewer in the western basin of the Mediterranean, where the Phoenicians and Etruscans had already established themselves. Finally, if account is taken of climate, vegetation possibilities, and of the ' midland sea,' it is found that the Greek colonies were so placed that the modes of life characteristic of Greece could be practised with little or no change : they could produce their grain, wine, and oil ; pasture their flocks of sheep and goats ; fish and trade by sea. There is, in fact, a remarkable correspondence between the distribution of Greek colonies and that of Mediterranean climate, and in Greece itself Greek civilisation gradually weakened on the

[1] See below, Chapter VIII.
[2] See below, Chapter V.

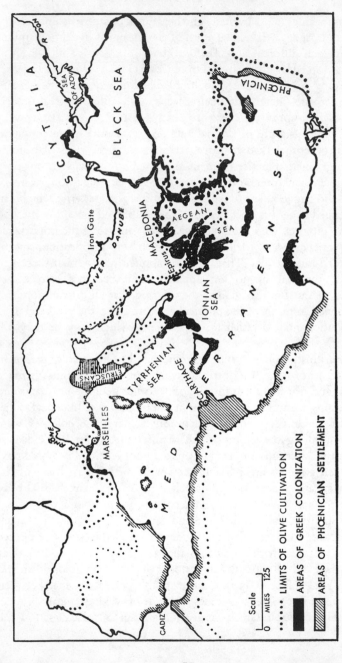

FIG. I   The Mediterranean World from the 7th to the 5th century B.C.

Scale

0   MILES   125

......   LIMITS OF OLIVE CULTIVATION

▓▓▓   AREAS OF GREEK COLONIZATION

▒▒▒   AREAS OF PHŒNICIAN SETTLEMENT

SCYTHIA

RIVER DON

SEA OF AZOV

BLACK SEA

Iron Gate

RIVER DANUBE

MACEDONIA

Epirus

AEGEAN SEA

PHŒNICIA

MEDITERRANEAN SEA

IONIAN SEA

CARTHAGE

ETRUSCANS

TYRRHENIAN SEA

MARSEILLES

RHÔNE

CADIZ

margins of this climatic province. On the other hand, although Mediterranean modes of life, without much modification, could be followed on the coasts of Portugal, Greek colonists did not settle so far westwards, and it is reasonable to conclude that they were reluctant to enter the tidal waters which lay beyond the Strait of Gibraltar.

Finally, there is one other aspect of history which stands closely related to geography. In the present-day countryside, as on the large-scale topographic maps which are now available in many countries, features alike of historical and geographical interest are everywhere interrelated. The conception of the countryside or the large-scale map as a 'palimpsest' or document, which, rightly deciphered by the expert, yields an abundant return alike to the geographer seeking to explain the present patterns, and to the historian interested in the surviving testimony of the past, illustrates concretely how mutually interdependent these two cognate studies can be. Armed with maps, the geographer, almost of necessity, must work 'in the field' in furtherance of his studies; in the open air also the historian can equally find grist to his mill. If the latter is studying, for example, prehistoric or Roman routes, hill-top camps of the Early Iron Age, or dykes and ramparts of the Dark Ages such as the remarkable Offa's Dyke, medieval abbeys or sheep-walks, river navigation, and so on, he may add both realism and precision to his narrative by direct observation 'in the field.' Of Grant Allen, whose book, *Town and Country in England*, showed a century ago a shrewd appreciation of the contemporary countryside as an historical palimpsest, it was written : [1]

It was a pleasant thing to go a walk with him. The country was to him a living being, developing under his eyes, and the history of its past was to be discovered from the conditions of the present.

And we may add that, in so far as man's achievement in modifying the face of the land forms a legitimate part of history, this particular history can be understood only if it is set against the relatively unchanging physical background.

The geography behind history can no longer be conceived as the hidden hand which directs human history, except perhaps during man's initial and prolonged phase of Old Stone Age culture. But in the course of cultural history in the broad sense, of economic and social history, and of political, military, and naval history, above all, *genius loci*

[1] Preface, by F. York Powell, to *Town and Country in England* (1901).

plays a continual part. The geographical way of thinking in terms of distinctive regions with their limited opportunities to man, and in terms of distributions in place, provides an auxiliary approach to these branches of history. Although we may well believe that, in the past, peoples understood only imperfectly the world around them, and fashioned their material culture by resort to trial and error ; although, too, their will and ability to adapt their world or to adjust themselves to it were continually changing : it is of obvious importance that in any reconstruction of the past this physical world should be examined with the same care that is lavished on literary sources. This geographical study involves the scrutiny of many maps, plans, and charts, and the use of much written material. It involves, too, wherever practicable, investigation ' in the field.' There are times, therefore, when the student of history should righteously forsake the library desk and, map in hand, stride forth into the world about him, the ins and outs of which may sometimes contain clearer clues to the past than do the musty manuscripts and the official records from which he draws the material, if not the inspiration, for his epic tale.

CHAPTER II

Old Maps as Historical Documents

> History . . . is exceedingly difficult to follow without maps . . . and,
> it may be whispered, geography untouched by the human element is
> dull to an extraordinary degree, duller even than mapless history, and
> that, the Dodo said, was the driest thing that it knew.
>
> SIR CHARLES CLOSE, *The Map of England* (1932)

OF COURSE, in his attempts at field investigation the historian is at the
disadvantage that the countryside has changed in many respects since
the period which he is studying. He is not permitted to use
H. G. Wells's time machine, to enable him to see it as it actually was
then. Inevitably he is concerned in the main, if not exclusively, with
literary and other materials which have survived from that stretch of
the past which interests him. And among such materials must be
included maps.

Old maps take many forms : they may be plans of cities, charts of
sea coasts and estuaries, cartularies of landed estates, or topographic
delineations of land areas. These clearly engage the interest of historians and geographers alike, and their study calls for a combination
of the methods and viewpoints of each. Maps can be conceived of,
and studied in several quite different ways. They may be properly
regarded, and so assessed, as works of art [1]—at best as things of colour,
skill, form, and beauty. They may alternatively be studied attentively
for their purely cartographic interest. The main question which then
arises is : how has the map-maker carried out his task and with what
skill and with what success ? Such an inquiry falls to the specialist
field of historical cartography. A third approach to an old map—the
one which concerns us here—is that of the student who conceives it as

---

[1] See, for example, 'the reproductions of twenty maps of historical and
artistic interest, suitable for framing' contained in *Early Maps of the British Isles
A.D. 1000–1579*, with an introduction by G. R. Crone (Royal Geographical
Society, 1962).

a source of information contemporaneous with the time of its production. Thus the historical geographer may seek to bring grist to his mill and will have first to consider the map's reliability as a source of evidence. By such means also the regional historian, in his search for knowledge about such past matters as the availability of roads, the extent of enclosed farmland, or the number and location of mines and quarries, is no less an interested party.

The value of old maps as documents useful for the reconstruction of the past depends necessarily on how much they depict and on how accurately they do this. For virtually all periods of history some maps have survived to record, however imperfectly, certain features of past geography. The work of Claudius Ptolemy—he lived in the 2nd century A.D.—for centuries provided the basis for maps of the known world and its major regions (Fig. 8, p. 26). Although many maps were drawn on the scientific basis which he provided, they nevertheless embodied many errors—of location, distance, and the shape of areas of land and sea.[1] The medieval portolan charts of the Mediterranean Sea and the later charts, giving sailing directions, produced in Holland, were accurate enough to be useful in practical navigation.[2] Plans of important cities of Europe, so well drawn as to yield evidence of their earlier form and extent, are notably offered in Braun and Hogenberg's *Civitates Orbis Terrarum*, which was published at Cologne, 1573–1613. In England, John Speed's plans of cities [3] have a similar value. A different genre of map, which gives detailed information of the road system of England as it existed nearly three centuries ago, is that contained in John Ogilby's *Britannia, Volume the First* which appeared in 1675. As to topographic maps proper, an early outstanding achievement was the map of the Rhine valley which was edited by Martin Waldseemüller and published at Strasbourg in 1513.

Few of the early maps approached modern standards, which require accurate representation of distances and of heights above mean sea-level and the use of carefully distinguished symbols. This is because it was not until the 18th century that cartography, as an exact science, was born. It is only then, with an increasing interest and competence in survey and cartography, that topographic maps of sufficient quality, detail, and precision for the purposes of history become available, at

[1] G. R. Crone, *Maps and their Makers: an Introduction to the History of Cartography* (1953), p. 20.

[2] E. G. R. Taylor, *The Haven-Finding Art* (1956).

[3] John Speed, *Theatre of the Empire of Great Britain* (London, 1611–12).

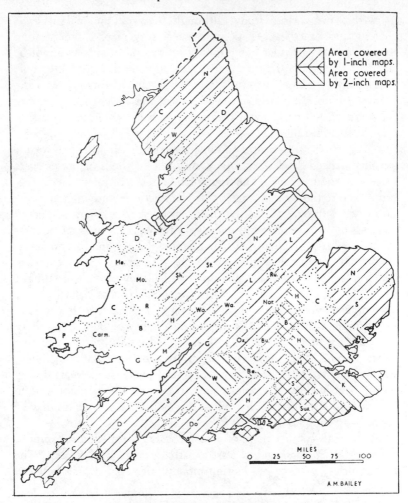

FIG. 2 Coverage of the counties of England by large-scale
topographic maps in the 18th century.

least in Western Europe. In France the work of the four Cassinis,
whose lives spanned the period 1625–1845, and in the Austrian Low
Countries that of Lieutenant-General Count Joseph de Ferraris,
achieved new and scientific standards in the cartographic representation
of those countries. In England, to which this discussion will be
limited, the half century (1750–1800) before the Ordnance Survey
published its first maps witnessed the appearance of numerous county

maps that merit close study, although they are unequal in scale, content, and exactness. Among these county maps those of John Rocque are of particular geographical interest, although it cannot be said that their value has as yet been definitively assessed.[1] Rocque, who described himself variously as a chorographer, topographer, and even geographer, and died in the year 1762, was a Huguenot emigrant from France and he brought originality as well as skill to his task of map-making in England.

Of course the 18th-century county maps of Britain, those of Rocque included, lacked geodetic accuracy, since the methods of survey were somewhat rudimentary. The triangulation of the country had scarcely begun before the creation in 1791 of what became known later as the Ordnance Survey. Certainly they reflect shortcomings in survey methods and show technical defects, as for example inexact orientation.[2] Evaluation of these maps on cartographic ground has, however, obscured somewhat their substantial value as contemporary documents. The features of the human geography which they provide are usually clear. The student must necessarily use these maps as critically as he does other contemporary material literary in character. It is found, for example, that in Rocque's map of the county of Berkshire a sharp and unlikely break in the area of cultivated land occurs where two sheets adjoin. This may result from error in representation, but it should be noted that the survey was spread over several years during which land-use changes might have occurred. Where for certain counties more than one independent survey is available, details may be checked by comparison.

Eighteenth-century maps on a useful scale give an almost complete coverage of England and at least a partial coverage of Wales. The Royal Society of Arts, by offering money prizes and medals between

[1] The best introduction to, and appreciation of, Rocque and his work is John Varley's 'John Rocque, Engraver, Surveyor, Cartographer and Map Seller,' *Imago Mundi*, edited by Leo Bagrow, V, 1948, pp. 83–91. This article contains a list of Rocque's publications. Sir H. G. Fordham might appear to have under-estimated Rocque's work and not to have studied it closely : see his depreciatory remarks in his *Studies in Carto-Bibliography*, Clarendon Press, Oxford, 1914, p. 86. L. D. Stamp in *The Land of Britain*, 2nd ed., 1950, p. 50, suggested that the representation of the enclosed fields on Rocque's map of Surrey is ' diagrammatic.' In contrast, Dr E. C. Willatts's *Middlesex and the London Region*, Report 79 of the Land Utilization Survey of Great Britain, 1937, p. 283, believed that Rocque's map of Middlesex (1754) ' gives an excellent representation of the surface utilization . . . in the middle of the eighteenth century.'

[2] Cf. Sir Charles Close, *The Map of Britain* (1932), p. 31.

the years 1759 and 1809 for county maps drawn on a scale of one inch
to the mile, did much to stimulate map-making,[1] the financial support
for such enterprise coming largely from landed patrons in the counties.
Actually in the course of the 18th century every county of England,
excepting only Cambridgeshire, was surveyed on either this or a larger
scale (Fig. 2). Unlike the Cassini maps of France, which were based
on the triangulation of the whole country, these county maps
lacked a standard form—the result of the uncoordinated private
enterprise which produced them. For these reasons their use as
a basis for determining distributions over the whole country is
virtually precluded. Their value, however, for regional studies
remains, and for a number of counties they have been put to good
service.[2]

The 18th-century county maps provide information, in varying
degrees incomplete, about the principal elements of the human
geography—the settlements, the land use, and other aspects of the
economy. Careful analysis of this material can give precision to
interpretations of 18th-century geography based on literary and sta-
tistical sources, and reveals the predominantly rural English countryside
before it was subjected to the rapid and remarkable changes associated
with the Industrial Revolution.

To particularise, the 18th-century maps illuminate in the several
counties some or all of the following aspects of their geography : the
distribution of land used for cultivation, pasture, woods, parks, and
commons ; the extent of enclosed fields and the sporadic survival of
the traditional open-field system of husbandry ; the administrative-
territorial areas of the counties and their parishes—the former often
being shown to have detached ' island ' areas in neighbouring counties ;
the distribution of country mansions ; villages, hamlets, farms, towns,
and ports—some of the two last-named being sometimes shown on
inset plans ; the canal system ; and the road pattern—here the maps
usually show clearly where the roads pass through enclosed or open
country, and where they have been improved under the operation of

---

[1] Awards totalling 460, four gold medals, three silver medals, and one silver
palette, were made to the makers of twelve county maps and one of North Wales.
See Sir H. T. Wood's account in the *Journal of the Royal Society of Arts*, vol. LX
(1911–12), pp. 268–9. See also Sir H. G. Fordham, *Some Notable Map-Makers of
the Sixteenth, Seventeenth and Eighteenth Centuries and their Work* (Cambridge,
1929), p. 73.

[2] For example, by H. C. K. Henderson, ' Our Changing Agriculture : the
Adur Basin of Sussex,' *Journal of the Ministry of Agriculture*, 43 (1936), p. 627.

Fig. 3 The distribution of arable land in Berkshire c. 1761 (based on John Rocque's survey).

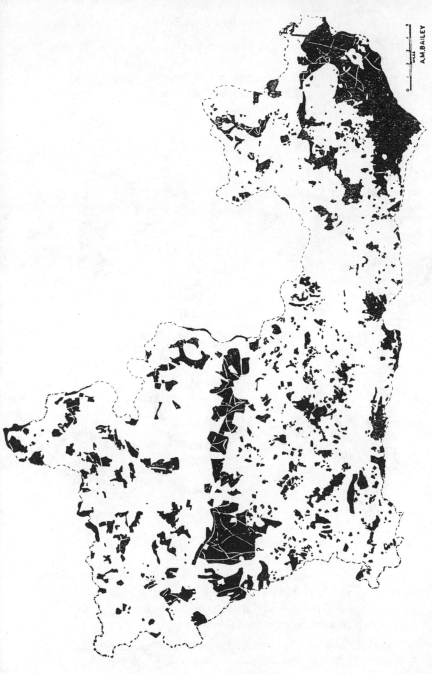

FIG. 4 The distribution of woodland, heath, and commons in Berkshire *c.* 1761 (based on John Rocque's survey).

A.M. BAILEY

Turnpike Acts. Lastly, the sites of mines and quarries are usually indicated.[1]

A selection of illustrations shows the range of geographical information obtainable from the 18th-century county maps of England. Figs. 3, 4, and 5 are based on Rocque's 'Actual Survey of Berkshire':

Fɪɢ. 5   The parish of Coleshill, Berkshire (after John Rocque).

this was drawn on a scale of two inches to the mile and published in eighteen sheets in 1761. What gives particular value to Rocque's surveys—notably those of London and its environs, Surrey, Middlesex, Shropshire, and Berkshire—is not only their large scale, which compares with the two-and-a-half-inch to the mile maps of the Ordnance Survey, which have become available only since 1947, but the fact that

[1] For a fuller discussion, see W. G. East, 'Land Utilization in England at the End of the Eighteenth Century,' *The Geographical Journal*, vol. lxxxix (1937), pp. 156–72.

they distinguish by appropriate symbols the different agricultural uses of the land—arable, pasture, meadow, woodland, parkland, orchards, and commons. This differentiation marked an innovation, for usually only woodlands, parks, and commons were shown. It is true that arable lands were depicted on William Roy's map of Scotland, prepared by compass survey on a scale of one inch to a thousand yards during the years 1747–55, but this pioneer map was not published.[1] And the Ordnance Survey, although its first sponsored publication, a map of Kent and part of Essex published in 1801, portrayed a range of land uses, did not adopt the practice of showing arable and pasture.

Figs. 3 and 4 show, on the basis of Rocque's survey, the distribution of cultivated land and of woodland, heath, and commons in Berkshire, while Fig. 5 reproduces photographically Rocque's delineation of one of its parishes—Coleshill.[2] It will be noted in this last figure how his choice of symbols distinguishes arable from pasture land and how he represented the compact village and the outlying farms of this parish.

A further illustration of the value of these old maps may be given from William Forrest's *Map of the Shire of Lanark*, which was based on surveys carried out in 1806–8 and published, on a scale of one and a half inches to the mile, at Edinburgh in 1816.[3] It clearly depicts areas of moss and woodland, settlements, and communications, as well as coal-workings, ironworks, mills, and quarries. It was not a faultless survey—indeed it is known that Forrest omitted to mark a few farms and estimated inaccurately the height of hills—and it gives little clue to the extent of arable and pasture land. Nevertheless it is singularly helpful, being precise about woodland and moss and throwing light on the extent and distribution of enclosure of farmland, as Fig. 6 illustrates.

Apart from county maps drawn on relatively large scales, smaller-scale maps, which both historians and geographers have found useful, are contained in the county agricultural reports which began to appear at the end of the 18th century. It may be recalled that these surveys were sponsored by the newly formed Board of Agriculture

[1] See A. C. O'Dell, 'A View of Scotland in the Middle of the Eighteenth Century,' *The Scottish Geographical Magazine*, vol. lxix, no. 2 (1953), pp. 58–63, for maps of land use in Scotland based on Roy's survey.

[2] On the more recent land use of Berkshire, see *The Land of Britain*, edited by L. D. Stamp, Part 78 Berkshire, by J. Stephenson, with a historical section by W. G. East, 1936.

[3] W. G. East, 'Land Utilisation in Lanarkshire at the End of the Eighteenth Century,' *The Scottish Geographical Magazine*, vol. 53 (March 1937), pp. 89–110.

and Internal Improvement, which was established in 1793 under the presidency of Sir John Sinclair and with Arthur Young as secretary. The object of the surveys was to discover 'the cultivation of the surface, and the resources to be derived from it.' About a third of the surveys included coloured maps drawn on scales of between four and six miles to the inch. Admittedly experimental and crude, these maps were generalised sketches designed to show regional contrasts of several kinds, especially of soil and land use, of a kind not attempted in the later Ordnance Survey maps.

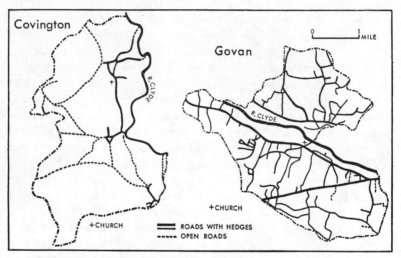

FIG. 6 Enclosed land in two Lanarkshire parishes *c.* 1808
(based on William Forrest's map).

The value of soil maps to the historian is self-evident for their relevance to the varied agricultural uses of the land and to the facilities of road transport in days before road engineering provided reliable surfaces. These maps attempt to indicate the pattern of soils as a farmer would distinguish them : strong loams, clay marls, rich friable loams, sands, and gravels are among the categories referred to. The counties of Suffolk, Staffordshire, Nottinghamshire, Oxfordshire, and Sussex were illustrated by such soil maps and, even if they were somewhat 'superficial and imperfect at best' (as the Rev. A. Young styled his map of Sussex), they nevertheless repay study.

In their attempts to distinguish regionally the uses of the land the county report maps have another historical interest. Thus Robert

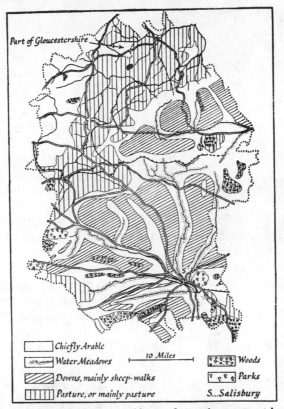

FIG. 7   Land use in Wiltshire (drawn from Thomas Davis's map,
1794 and, with slight modifications, 1813).

Lowe's map of Nottingham (1794) indicates 'coal and limestone
districts,' as it also throws light on the extent of enclosed fields and on
the use of regional names such as Vale of Belvoir and Nottinghamshire
Weald. John Middleton's map of Middlesex (1798) suggests the
location and extent of the 'nursery grounds and gardens' which lay
beyond built-up London to the west and to the north. Fig. 7, which
is drawn from Thomas Davis's map of Wiltshire (six miles to the inch)
and published in his report of 1794, may be noted as one of the best
of these maps.   Alongside his report, which was based on careful
survey, his map depicts boldly the land-use pattern, for water-meadow,
arable, pasture, woods, and parks, which characterised this relatively
prosperous and populous county where good markets, especially that
of London, made good farmers.

CHAPTER III

Geographical Position

Where is Africa ?

NOEL COWARD, *Cavalcade*

' WHERE is Africa ? ' inquired the servant girl in *Cavalcade* of the hero
returned from the Boer War, and it may be recalled that she received
an inadequate answer. At first sight the question seems easily solvable
with the aid of an atlas or, better still, a globe. But can questions
about position be answered merely in terms of latitude and longitude,
these convenient devices, useful alike to cartographers and to navigators, which impose a frame of reference on maps of the earth's surface ?

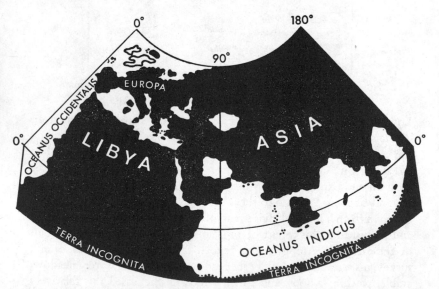

FIG. 8   The World *c.* A.D. 150, according to Ptolemy.
The British Isles are left white.

Certainly we may well believe that the disposition of the lands and the seas remained virtually stable during the minute period of human history. Wegener's brilliant hypothesis of 'continental drift,' which explains the present arrangement of the continents as the result of their disruption and movement away from an original unitary land area, need not concern us here, since it relates, not to human history, but to the more ample phases of geological time. Still less need we concern ourselves with the ever-changing map of subsequent geological periods. Throughout historical times the positional characteristics of any Place are of some importance, since, together with other geographical attributes, they had some bearing on its history. Reflection will suggest that position is not merely an absolute concept, which can be defined mathematically, but also a relative concept, for men have always lived in a changing world. The position of a Place, therefore, is both a variable and a stable factor of geography : only in part is it a natural fact—something which is given and changeless. In so far as it is variable in relation to a changing world, position must be correctly assessed for different periods of history. We cannot safely assume for the past the positional value which a Place today enjoys—not unless we would commit one of the more heinous of historical misdemeanours.

Position, then, if on the one hand absolute, is on the other relative, but relative to what ? Above all, to what the Greeks called the *œkumene* —that is, the known and habitable world—which was by no means coincident historically with the true extent of the earth's surface.

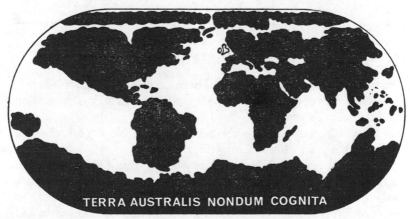

FIG. 9   The World in A.D. 1570, according to Ortelius.
The British Isles are left white.

Compare, for example, the world as it was known in the heyday of
the Roman Empire with that known to cosmographers after the great
age of geographical discovery (Figs. 8 and 9). Since the time of
Ortelius' map the bounds of the known world have been extended
still farther : the salient features of the land and water areas of the
earth are now almost fully known, for at least the main outlines of the
Polar regions have been drawn. The position of a Place at any time
is affected, too, by the extent to which the known lands were populous
or unsettled, civilised or barbarous. Finally, the degree to which a

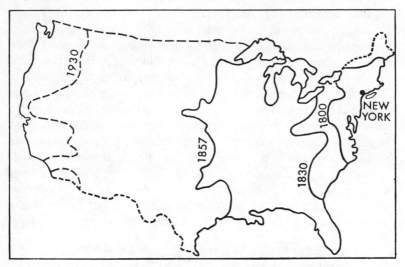

FIG. 10   Areas reached by a week's travel from New York in
1800, 1830, and 1857, and by three days' travel in 1930.

given position is marginal or central depends in part on its accessibility,
and this in turn changes from age to age as the means of communication
and transport change.

Note, for example, how the accessibility of New York changed
between the years 1800 and 1930 (Fig. 10).

We may say that inherent in any Place were certain positional
possibilities which were utilised in varying degrees at different times.
Our own islands afford an excellent illustration of this idea. Their
position has often been extolled as a permanent and valuable asset, and
used to explain certain facets of their history. That position, however,
has certainly not been stable throughout history. The insularity of

Britain, for example, is not as agelong as its human history : during many millennia—which correspond with the Palaeolithic, or Old Stone, Age and its successor the Mesolithic period—Britain remained firmly welded to the continent (Fig. 11). Today, it is true, the British Isles enjoy a distinctly advantageous position. Close to, yet detached from, the continent with which they are related by geological struc-

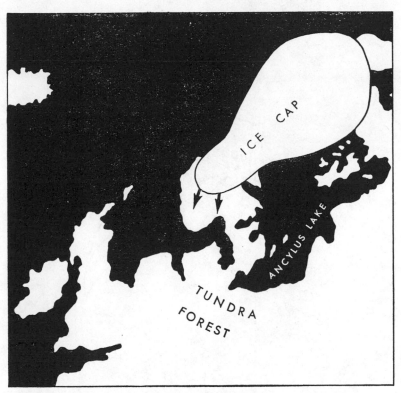

FIG. 11   Britain attached to the Continent, *c.* 7500 B.C.
After L. D. Stamp.

ture, they occupy that position in Europe which lies most advanced towards North America. The way stood open to them, once the sea routes had been explored and secured, not only to the New World, South Africa, and the Far East, but also to the more local semi-enclosed seas—the North Sea, the Baltic, and the Mediterranean. No land area lay immediately westwards of the British Isles athwart the direct sea-ways to North America, but other states of western Europe, notably

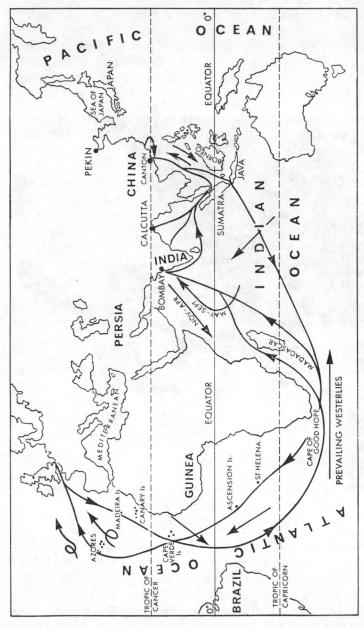

Fig. 12 Sailing Routes between Britain and the Far East.
See the reference to this map on p. 171.

Portugal, Spain, France, and Holland, alike enjoyed a western frontage to the North Atlantic and played their parts in the commerce and settlement of the Americas. For the oceanic route to the Cape of Good Hope and the Far East (Fig. 12), both Portugal and Spain were better placed than the British Isles, an advantage which the former did not fail to exploit.

It may be remarked that the extent to which position alone is a significant factor in history presents a nice question. In some respects, for example, the position of Ireland was superior to that of the greater, more productive, and more populous island, yet it was the latter, and more particularly England, which took advantage of the opportunities offered by the new location which the British Isles assumed subsequently to the geographical discoveries of the late 15th and early 16th centuries. The striking feature of that new location was that the British Isles found themselves at the centre of the known and inhabited land hemisphere [1] as well as at the gateway into Europe from the New World. As a result, Britain ceased to be just

> . . . this paltry little isle
> With acres few and weather vile.

In contrast, the position of the British Isles in the early stages of their history was much less enviable. For many thousands of years these islands stood remote from, and marginal to, the most highly developed civilisations of the time. They formed a veritable cul-de-sac at the western end of the Eurasian land mass, as did the Japanese islands at its eastern end. Two local sea routes, it is true, passed through their home waters. The narrow seas between Britain and Ireland afforded an alternative route from south-west Europe to Scandinavia and Iceland. Similarly, the English Channel was a thoroughfare for ships sailing between the Mediterranean and the North Sea or the Baltic. But essentially, our islands stood at a terminus of routes. To the west lay the trackless Atlantic : even after the Vikings had crossed it for the first time in the 10th century, it remained a barrier frontier until the time of Columbus. To the north, also, beyond Iceland and western Scandinavia, seas which were frozen over except in summer formed a blind alley (Fig. 13). From the 11th century onwards southern Greenland alone, which was colonised by the Danes, became a distant

[1] On this point, see Sir H. J. Mackinder, *Britain and the British Seas* (1902), chap. ii.

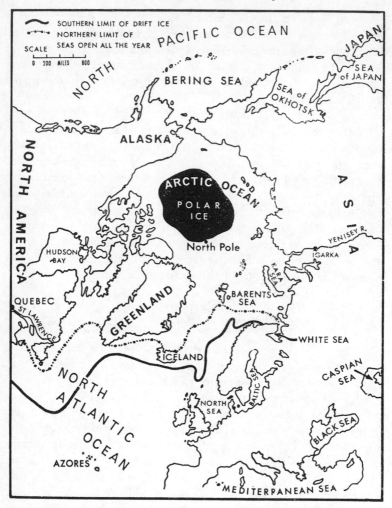

FIG. 13   The northern front of the Old and New Worlds.

outpost of European civilisation on the margin of the Arctic Ocean. There were no practicable routes north-eastwards or north-westwards to India and China and their fabled wealth, such as cosmographers conceived and explorers sought in the 16th century, and even the relatively short passage to the White Sea was opened up only in the reign of Queen Elizabeth I.

If we throw back our minds as far as the third millennium before

Christ, when civilised ways of life were slowly spreading into the Mediterranean peninsulas and into central Europe, we find that the British Isles, together with western France and northern Europe, then remained among the most backward and unprogressive areas of the Old World (Fig. 14). Successive cultures of the Neolithic, Bronze, and Early Iron Ages reached Britain late, and in somewhat enfeebled forms. Ireland, it is true, putting to good use its resources of gold and copper, nurtured an original and flourishing civilisation during the

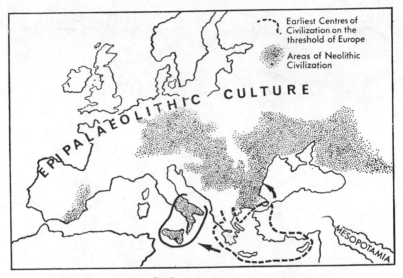

FIG. 14   Areas of culture in Europe, *c.* 2500–2000 B.C.

early Bronze Age which for a time reversed the east–west flow of cultural currents. This fact does not undermine the generalisation that the British Isles, despite their cultural individualities, were actually outliers of cultures which had matured on the continent. In so far as European civilisation depended during the Neolithic and Bronze Ages on diffusion of peoples and ideas from some of the earliest centres of civilisation [1]—namely Egypt, Mesopotamia, Crete, and the Ægean world—clearly the British Isles occupied a remote and unfavourable position. Not only did they stand far off in actual mileage, but, given the means of communication of the time, they were relatively inaccessible. England stood no farther from Egypt as the crow flies than

[1] See below, Chapter IX.

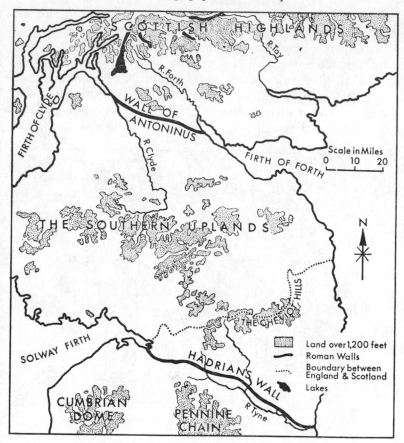

Fig. 15 The Roman walls and the Anglo-Scottish boundary.

did Almeria in south-eastern Spain, yet Neolithic civilisation reached the latter some five hundred years or so earlier than it reached England. It may have been diffused into Almeria by way of the Mediterranean or the open steppe lands of north Africa ; it reached Britain via continental Europe, where—owing to extensive forests, marshes, and mountain obstacles—penetration was less easy and less rapid.

Nor, during the Roman period, when the Mediterranean Sea formed the axis of Græco-Roman civilisation, was the position of the British Isles other than excentric (Fig. 8). The centre of gravity of the Roman Empire, in respect of population and commerce, lay in Italy itself and in the eastern basin of the inland sea—in Egypt, Syria, and the coastlands of Asia Minor. Only the southern part of Britain, south of the Central Valley of Scotland, was deemed worth conquering by the Roman emperors, and the conquest of Ireland, lightly contemplated by the Roman general Agricola,[1] was never undertaken. It was rather for strategical reasons than for its intrinsic wealth and importance that Britain was occupied, since some of the peoples of southern England had supported their kinsfolk in Gaul against Rome. The two walls which were built by the Roman legions across the ' waists ' of England and Scotland were defences on the north-west frontier of the Roman Empire, beyond which less civilised ways of life persisted (Fig. 15). To a Roman legionary, service there on guard against ' the Picts, the Caledonians and other Scots,' must have been comparable with that of British soldiers on the North-West frontier of India—virtual exile in the wilderness. Similarly, in the days when its glory had long passed away, Greece seemed to officials sent there from Constantinople ' an utter hole.'

It is not without interest that the position of Ireland, if we can believe Tacitus, was assessed by the Romans more highly than that of Britain. ' Ireland,' he wrote, ' lying in the mid-way between Spain and Britain, and likewise very convenient for the Gallic Sea, would, if conquered, unite the strongest parts of the Empire by its great advantages ; . . . in a higher degree, the approaches and harbours of Ireland are known by merchants.' Whatever its inaccuracies, this statement is geographically suggestive. Eastern, if not southern, Britain faced the less developed northern part of Gaul and the ' barbarian ' or non-Roman world which lay beyond the Rhine. Southern and eastern Ireland was reached, with the aid of the prevailing sou'-westers, by coastwise sailings along the coasts of Portugal, Spain, and France, or more directly by short sea passages from Brittany via Cornwall. This route, or at least parts of it, seems, on good archaeological evidence, to have been followed for some two thousand years or more before the Roman Empire (Fig. 27, p. 67).

Britain long remained a marginal fragment of Europe, from which it received peoples, languages, its religion, and some at least of its political institutions. The insularity of Britain and Ireland in no sense spelt isolation ; nor did it condition political unification. At different times Britain became, not so much aloof and insular, as part of wider political units, the parts of which were held together by use of the

[1] He thought that Ireland could be subdued with the aid of seven or eight thousand troops !

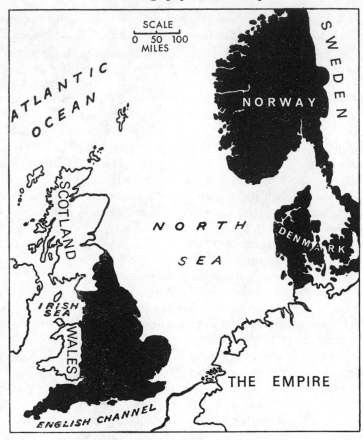

FIG. 16   The kingdom of Canute, A.D. 1014–1035.
*Note its relation to the semi-enclosed North Sea,
the Irish Sea, and the English Channel.*

sea-ways across either the North Sea or the English Channel (Figs. 16 and 17).   Nor did the insularity of Britain evoke at once a seafaring population.   It is something of an exaggeration to suggest, as some German writers do, that prior to the late 16th century England remained a land of peasants who lived aloof from the sea, and that its foreign trade was entirely in the hands of aliens, notably the Hansards and the Venetians.   Yet this view contains a large element of truth. The first seamen, in historical times at least, who seemed at home in the local waters of the North Sea, the Channel, and the Irish Sea, were not Britishers, but peoples from continental shores—in turn Anglo-

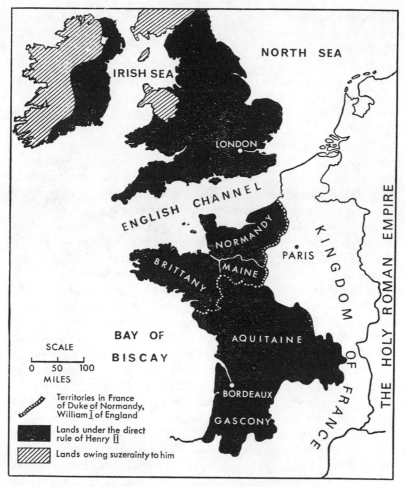

FIG. 17 The kingdom of Henry II at its maximum extent.
Note its relation to the narrow waters.

Saxons, Frisians, and Vikings. But during part at least of the later
Middle Ages, English kings held mastery of the Channel, and during
the 15th century, if not earlier, English fishermen were sailing from
Bristol to Iceland, and English ships were trading with Ireland, the
Iberian peninsula, France, and the Baltic. It is true, however, that
English enterprise lagged behind that of Portugal and Spain during
the great age of discovery, although it eventually played some part.

37

But it was not until the defeat of the Armada in 1588 that England became a strong sea-state, ready to exploit the possibilities presented by the new oceanic routes.

Let us turn to an illustration of the importance of geographical position at the dawn of history (Fig. 18). No one can question the fact that Crete, the Cyclades Islands, and Troy were the areas where civilisation first appeared on the threshold of Europe. If, as some hold, this civilisation—which included the practice of cultivation, pastoral farming, writing, city life, metallurgy, architecture, and other arts—arose spontaneously in Crete, it is certainly difficult to assign much importance to geographical factors. As a recent exponent of this view, A. J. Toynbee, wrote : 'Crete, like the rest of the Ægean world, is bare, barren, rocky, mountainous, and broken into fragments by the estranging sea.' He is able to explain the precocious civilisation of the Ægean lands only as the remarkable human response to physical conditions of unusual difficulty. How far this interpretation gives due weight to the geographical facts we need not discuss here, although we should note that Crete is the largest and most fruitful of the many islands of the Ægean Sea. But if we adopt the more generally accepted view, which had behind it the authority of Sir Arthur Evans, and believe that Crete received its first quickening impulse from Egypt, we must be struck at once by the relevance of the positional factor. For the civilisation which had flourished in Egypt and Mesopotamia [1] earlier than that of Crete was certainly not without effects on neighbouring lands. There are hints of early trade relations between Egypt and Syria, and between Egypt and the island of Naxos, which is a member of the Cyclades group. So also Mesopotamia had relations with Syria and with Asia Minor, near the north-western shores of which stood Pergamum (Troy). When we remember, too, that Crete, a detached fragment of Europe, stands nearer to Egypt than any other part of Europe, and that the Cyclades, together with other island groups, form stepping-stones between Asia Minor and Crete, it is tempting to conclude that the geographical position of Crete and the Cyclades Islands was a significant factor in the genesis and development of Ægean civilisation.

The fortunes of Crete between the years 3000 and 1900 B.C. indicate clearly how its relative position changed. If at first it stood marginally to the civilised lands of Egypt, Syria, and Asia Minor, it became later,

---

[1] See below, Chapter IX.

as a result of its sea power and commerce, the centre of the eastern basin of the Mediterranean (Fig. 18). Its maritime relations extended westwards to Sicily and southern Italy, eastwards to Pergamum, Cyprus, and Syria, and south-eastwards to Egypt. With the spread of civilisation from Crete to the Greek mainland, Crete lost and Greece won this central position in the east Mediterranean. Greece, in turn, abandoned this position only later when Rome secured the central position in the Mediterranean for Italy, which seemed to occupy this by nature. But before the establishment of the Roman Empire, the

FIG. 18   The position of Crete, Troy, and the Cyclades Islands.
The circle shown has its centre in central
Crete and a radius of about 500 miles.

position of Italy and Sicily was marginal rather than central in relation to the most civilised lands of that time.

Sicily, too, affords a striking illustration of how changes in relative position occur and affect history : [1] at first marginal to the civilised Ægean lands, it became and long remained central to the highly developed civilisation of the Mediterranean world, until the inland sea itself lost its central position with the opening up of the oceanic routes to the Americas and the Far East.

In conclusion, two further instances may be given to show the historical interest which attaches to the conception of geographical

[1] See, on Sicily, W. Gordon East, *An Historical Geography of Europe*, chap. xiv.

position. Why was it that the southern Low Countries, which we may equate with modern Belgium, were largely lacking in towns and relatively backward under the Roman Empire, yet became later, in the last centuries of the Middle Ages, the most populous, urbanised, and industrialised part of Europe ? Its position relative to the known world did not change between these two periods. The southern Low Countries fronted the English Channel and lay close both to Britain and the Baltic lands. At the earlier period, however, the southern Low Countries stood on the margins of the Roman Empire, the heartland of which lay in the Mediterranean lands, and beyond the Rhine stretched the relatively backward non-Roman or 'barbarian' world. At the later period the Baltic lands had been colonised and civilised chiefly by peoples from Gaul, and many seaports had been founded around the shores of the Baltic. Britain, too, had become a more populous and productive land. Moreover, developments in seamanship brought the Low Countries into direct relation, by way of the tidal sea, with flourishing Italian cities, notably Venice and Genoa. Many other considerations, it is true, are involved in any complete answer to our question : the fact that the Franks, who built up a great continental empire, aloof from the Mediterranean, had their geographical base astride the lower Rhine, is certainly a relevant factor. But it is clear that the relative position and accessibility of the Low Countries had improved since Roman times, and these positional advantages for industry and trade, formerly latent, could therefore be exploited.[1]

Finally, we may note how the origin of a great French city, Lyons, owed something to changes in relative position. This town, deliberately chosen by the Romans as the capital and route centre of Gaul, did not exist as a town in the Celtic Gaul which the Romans conquered. This is surprising for two reasons. First, because many of the cities of Roman Gaul—for example, Marseilles, Paris, Orleans, and Bourges— already existed prior to the Roman conquest, if only in somewhat rudimentary forms. Second, because the site of Lyons, at the junction of what are virtually three navigable rivers—the upper Rhône, the lower Rhône, and the Saône—seems almost predestined for a town and route centre. Not only does it stand at the convergence of the three waterways, each with its distinct conditions of navigation, but it commands landward passage along the Rhône and Saône valleys, and

---

[1] For a full account, see W. Gordon East, *op. cit.*, pp. 330–9.

routes which lead eastwards to Italy by way of passes across the western Alps.

The absence of Lyons among the towns of pre-Roman Gaul is explained by its relative position at that time. It appears that the river Saône formed a boundary between two Celtic peoples, the Ædui and the Allobroges, and since these peoples were frequently at war, the site which Lyons later occupied was scarcely suitable for the rise of a trading town. A frontier of friction is not the best milieu within which a civic society, dependent on wide regional relationships, can rise and flourish.

CHAPTER IV

Climate and History

The empire of climate is the first of all the empires.

MONTESQUIEU, *L'Esprit des Lois*

A CONSIDERABLE literature, in no small degree controversial in character, centres around the problem of past climates, and advocates are not lacking who argue the crucial importance of climatic changes as a partial explanation of the location of the first civilisations, the migrations of peoples, and even the rise and fall of empires. 'A favourable climate,' wrote Ellsworth Huntington, 'is an essential condition of high civilisation'; and another expert in this field, C. E. P. Brooks, asserted: 'The districts where civilisation began probably had at that time the most stimulating climate in the northern hemisphere.' In contrast to these views, the historian A. J. Toynbee maintained that 'the greater the ease of the environment, the weaker the stimulus towards civilisation.' The bearing of these views on the genesis of civilisation in Egypt, Mesopotamia, and north-west India, we shall examine in a later chapter.[1] Here we may note that the way in which climate directly affects man and his activities today raises a question to which no completely satisfactory answer can be given. That climate varies regionally, not only horizontally but also vertically, is a familiar fact, and it is a prime concern of the geographer to show not only the broad types of climate which occur from place to place, but also the varieties of local climate within a given climatic region at different altitudes, in different aspects, and so forth. How far can we claim, following Greek philosophers and Montesquieu, that climate has direct effects on man's physical, mental, and moral make-up? An able exponent of such direct influences of climate on man, and thus on the activities which fill the chronicles of his history, argued [2] that certain

[1] See below, Chapter IX.
[2] Ellsworth Huntington, *Civilization and Climate*, 2nd ed., 1922.

parts of the world enjoy today a climate which stimulates man to a maximum physical and mental effort. A certain seasonal temperature range, relative humidity, and day-to-day changes of weather are the factors which combine to produce this so-called ' ideal ' climate, which is found to be characteristic of western Europe and a great part, especially the north-eastern part, of the United States.

Acceptance of this view raises serious difficulties, even when allowance is made for the deadening effect on human effort of prolonged periods of excessive cold or of excessive heat, especially when this is coupled with a high degree of humidity. If it is true that the ideal climate occurs in western Europe and in North America, two major historical difficulties confront us. How was it that, under climatic conditions which are believed to have been broadly analogous to those of the present, European folk remained during the period between 5000 and 3000 B.C. amongst the most backward and sluggish of contemporary peoples ? How was it, too, that when Europeans reached North, as distinct from Central, America, they found there a population of Indians who lived still at the hunting stage, practised little cultivation, were ignorant of iron, and did not possess any beast of burden or any domesticated animal except the dog ? It would be rash to deny that climate acts directly and potently on man ; but it would be no less rash to pretend that in the present state of our knowledge many, if any, dependable generalisations can be made on this subject—which raises intricate problems for future research.

We can speak with more assurance about the indirect effects of climate on man. Climate affects man indirectly through its influence on vegetation, and thus through its influence on the nature and economic possibilities of his habitat. It stands, together with soil and relief, as one of the factors, and usually the chief, which condition in any place its ' *modes de vie.*' By this convenient phrase, which means ' the ways in which a livelihood is got,' French geographers indicate what is the most significant link between man and his physical environment, since, according to the physical equipment of any place, so will be suggested to man, within more or less rigid limits, particular means of livelihood, particular forms of economic activity. Consider two simple cases. Wide open stretches of the Afrasian steppe–desert belt— which are too arid for cultivation yet are covered sporadically by certain pasture grasses and contain scattered water holes or oases— suggest, and almost inevitably impose, the nomad's way of life. Or, again, consider an area in temperate latitudes—for example, in the

Mediterranean region—where lowland pastures, available only in the winter season, are juxtaposed to upland pastures available only during the hot season. In such an area nature suggested the idea of seasonal movement of stock, the historic practice known as transhumance.[1]

Climate, to repeat, is the chief among those physical agents which define within what limits and in what ways man can seek his livelihood. It is so, because all plants can grow only within certain climatic limits. Some, like the olive, can survive summer drought ; wheat requires a certain growing period free from frosts, which, by a careful breeding of plants, man has reduced to a minimum of about ninety days ; rice and citrus fruits require much moisture as well as heat ; and even grass, the food for stock, cannot survive extreme cold or summer drought. We have already noted that, although he cannot change climate, man can in many ways evade its rigorous control—by irrigation, drainage works, wind screens, and by plant breeding. As an essential aid, though also as a challenge, climate has always conditioned human activity. The variations of the seasons largely determined the farmer's calendar, and the local conditions of temperature and rainfall set limits to the food and vegetable raw materials which could be produced. The distribution of natural vegetation, too, corresponded broadly with climatic belts, and forests in particular provided in early times forbidding zones which confined man's movements.

We have indicated above that climatic changes throughout history have been postulated, and herein lies the crux of the subject for our present purpose. Should climate be grouped among the variable factors of geography, and is it therefore unsafe to assume for past periods the climates which at present obtain ? On what evidence does the belief in climatic change rest, and what is the nature of the changes which occurred ? Can we, having discovered them, correlate phases of climate with phases of history and prehistory ? Finally, are the ascertained changes of climate significant geographically, or only so to the climatologist ? In other words, were the changes of such a scale as to have produced important modifications of the vegetation and the habitability of particular places, and thus to have prompted changes in the human response ?

That there is nothing intrinsically improbable about the notion of climatic changes during history is suggested by two facts. First, many climatic changes, culminating in those of the last Ice Age, are known

[1] See below, Chapter VIII, pp. 117–18.

to have occurred during geological times. Second, in recent times, as meteorological records bear witness, a number of cyclical fluctuations of climate have taken place. The whole period of man's presence on the earth, which is estimated at 500,000 years, coincides with the later phases of the last Ice Age. Geologists recognise four main stages in the Quaternary (or last) glaciation in Europe and North America.

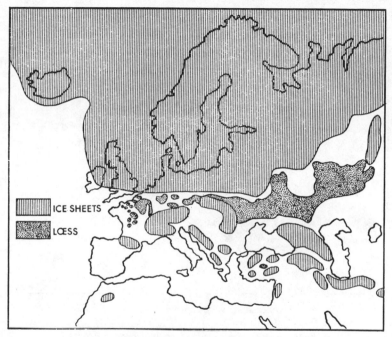

Fig. 19   Europe in the Great Ice Age.
*The Loess of the Danubian Basin
is not shown ; see below, Fig. 26.*

After each glacial onset, when glaciers extended southwards from Scandinavia into the North European Plain (see Fig. 19), an interglacial period of great length followed, when climate improved, becoming even warmer than today, and thus provided conditions suitable to human existence. The last stage of the Ice Age, the Würm phase, began about 40,000 B.C. and lasted in Sweden until about 6500 B.C., but small re-advances of the glaciers occurred in the sixth millennium (i.e. 6000–5000 B.C.). The earliest evidences of human species, which were other than the species *Homo sapiens*, the sole survivor today, may be dated at least as early as the interglacial period which preceded the Würm phase. The more recent periods of history which succeeded the disappearance of the Würm glaciers correspond with yet another interglacial period, in which we now live. How many millennia lie before us until the next glacial period sets in we cannot tell, but the probability of its eventual onset serves to remind us that we live in a world of changing climate.[1]

During the millennia between 18,000 and 8000 B.C., when the ice was disappearing from the North European Plain, the arrangement of

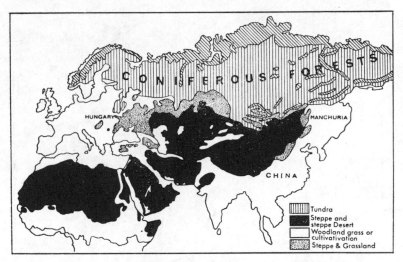

FIG. 20   A generalised vegetation map of the Old World.
Note the location of the steppe-desert belt, and how it separates Europe from central Africa and the monsoon lands of south-eastern Asia.

climatic belts in Europe was very different from that of today. The area of high pressure which now tends to lie over the Arctic Ocean then extended far south. As a result, the Atlantic rainstorms were deflected southwards from their present course, so that they passed eastwards across the Mediterranean and western Asia. These rainstorms were effective throughout at least the northern part of the present Afrasian steppe-desert belt (Figs. 20 and 21), as well as farther east—in Mesopotamia, Baluchistan, and the lower Indus valley.[2] This

[1] On post-glacial changes of climate in Britain, see Gordon Manley, *Climate and the British Scene*, Fontana Library, 1962, pp. 274–304.

[2] See below, Chapter IX, p. 131.

now arid belt then enjoyed, therefore, a moderate rainfall well distributed throughout the year ; as a result, it became an extensive grassland or rather savanna country, comparable with that which lies in Africa today on the southern margin of the deserts. Nor is there ground for scepticism about these former conditions of climate and

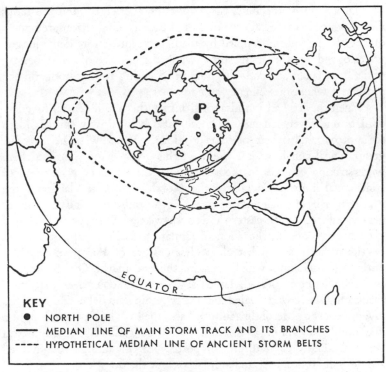

KEY
● NORTH POLE
── MEDIAN LINE OF MAIN STORM TRACK AND ITS BRANCHES
---- HYPOTHETICAL MEDIAN LINE OF ANCIENT STORM BELTS

FIG. 21   Storm tracks, past and present.
After Huntington, modified.

vegetation, since archaeological evidence corroborates the climatologist's deductions. From discoveries of cave drawings and of the bones of animals, the archaeologist has shown that the Afrasian steppe was formerly the habitat of many animal species which are found today not in arid areas but in grasslands, and that a number of tree species formerly existed there which would be sought in vain today under the ruling climatic conditions.[1]   Nor is there reasonable doubt that these

---

[1] See below, Chapter IX, pp. 138–9.

conclusions of the archaeologist relate to part, at least, of the long period when the ice was making its final retreat.

The bearing of these geographical conditions on the prehistory of the Afrasian steppe–desert belt can be briefly shown. During the wet period described above, groups of people, at the Palaeolithic (or Old Stone Age) stage of culture, lived in the grasslands by hunting. The alluvial valleys of the Nile, the Euphrates, the Tigris, and the Indus rivers, which became later the homes of the first civilisations, remained during this period unoccupied by man. Overgrown by dense jungle, waterlogged, and marshy, they were the resorts of wild beasts ; difficult to penetrate, and forbidding to hunting folk at home on the grasslands where movement was easy.

When the ice had withdrawn from southern and central Sweden, climate underwent change. The climatic belts slowly shifted north to approximately their present positions. What were in turn the geographical and historical effects of this great change ? First, there were striking changes in the vegetation cover : over wide areas of continental Europe, including the North European Plain and the southern half of Scandinavia, trees, both coniferous and deciduous, penetrated from south-eastern and south-western Europe and colonised extensively. The amelioration of climate had also its apparent effect on the hitherto somewhat changeless culture of European peoples ; during the millennia which separate the end of the Old Stone Age and the Neolithic period, let us say from *c.* 8000 to *c.* 3000 B.C., archaeologists have revealed on many shore and lake-side sites the inventiveness of Mesolithic culture,[1] so-called. These people sought a livelihood by hunting, fishing, and food-gathering, though still ignorant alike of agriculture, of pottery, of metallurgy, of civilised arts, and of all domesticated animals except the dog.

The northward shift of the climatic belts deprived the Afrasian grasslands of the Atlantic rainstorms. They suffered, as a consequence, gradual desiccation, so that the environment was transformed and a stern challenge was thrown down to its occupants. Instead of plentiful pasture, interspersed with trees, appeared dry wastes with intermittent, poor, xerophytic grasses, and occasional oases. The animal denizens of the grasslands met the new conditions by migrating widely. From North Africa, for example, they moved southwards, and northwards into Europe. The effects on man were no less striking, and it may

---

[1] See below, Chapter X, p. 150.

well be that climatic change explains the momentous change from the primitive food-collecting economy of hunting groups to the food-producing economy of the first civilised folk. If we may summarise briefly the now orthodox view,[1] we may say that the peoples of the steppe–desert belt were offered a threefold choice. They could emigrate in search of more familiar and congenial environments in the wake of the wild animals on which they depended for their food. They could stay where they were, in which case those who managed to survive the hard conditions would have to modify their way of life. Or lastly, they could think out a new kind of livelihood by means of cultivation and animal husbandry, in which case they could explore the possibilities of the formerly neglected riverine lands. Actually, it appears that all three courses were adopted by different groups. It must suffice to note here two remarkable results. One was that, alike on the margins of the valleys of the Nile, Euphrates, and Tigris, a Neolithic culture of villagers—who engaged in agriculture, possessed domesticated animals, made pottery, and showed skill in other crafts—appeared for the first time about the year 5000 B.C.[2] The other was the emergence of 'nomadism' as a new way of living within the steppe–desert belt. Nomadism means literally 'cattle-driving,' or the movement of flocks and herds from place to place in search of the scanty available pasture.

We may regard it as certain, therefore, that measurable changes of climate have taken place within the period of human history, although the nature of the alleged changes in particular areas and at particular times has been much disputed. Geographers, archaeologists, and historians, no less than climatologists, have joined issue on these problems of common interest, and clearly many difficulties arise in the attempt to evaluate and reconcile fragmentary evidence derived from different specialist studies. Some experts have been at great pains, not without some measure of success, to show that climate remained apparently stable since early historical times, or, arguing more cautiously, they sought merely to prove that the climate at a particular time was essentially that of today. For, we may note in passing, proof of this latter contention does not preclude fluctuations of climate between the selected date and the present. By a careful study of the climatic requirements of the date palm and of its distribution in

[1] See V. Gordon Childe, *The Most Ancient East* (1929), chap. ii., and A. J. Toynbee, *A Study of History*, vol. i (1934), pp. 302–5.

[2] See below, Chapter IX.

Biblical and present times, J. W. Gregory showed that the mean temperature of Palestine was approximately the same at both periods, but his argument did not exclude the possibility of changes in rainfall. Similarly, the question whether or not the Sahara and North Africa were wetter in Roman times than today has been much debated. Huntington argued that there was a distinctly wet phase, wetter than today, from 200 B.C. to A.D. 200, and that during the two succeeding centuries, which witnessed the decline of the Roman Empire, rainfall steadily decreased. He suggested, too, that this alleged climatic change between A.D. 200 and 400 was a contributory cause of the agrarian and social troubles in Italy, and even of the collapse of the Roman Empire itself. It must be admitted that some of the evidence on which this hypothesis rests is equivocal and unconvincing. It is not always safe to infer from the decay of cities, the abandonment of trade routes, and the disappearance of animals usually associated with moist grasslands that the rainfall of a semi-arid area has decreased. We know, for example, that elephants were numerous in North Africa in early Roman times and that they almost vanished soon after the fall of Rome. Their extinction, however, seems to have been due primarily to the Romans themselves, who used elephants in large numbers in warfare. Again, the remarkable eclipse of flourishing cities, such as Timgad in Tunisia and Palmyra in eastern Syria, both situated in areas now arid, may have resulted, in part at least, from the discontinuance of efforts necessary to discover, store, and distribute water, in which the Romans particularly excelled. On the other hand, the former conditions of rainfall in California, for which good evidence exists, may well be applicable, as Huntington argued, to the Mediterranean region, since southern California today enjoys a climate of Mediterranean type. If this argument is valid, then the rainfall conditions of North Africa between 200 B.C. and A.D. 400 followed the course stated above. The French historian Gsell, who studied North Africa with great care, believed that either the climate had not changed at all, or that it was *slightly* wetter in Roman times than it is today. In sum, the balance of evidence favours this latter conclusion of Gsell's. If this is sound, it would be rash to seek in the contemporary changes in rainfall an explanation of the economic, social, and political problems of the Roman Empire. It is not clear that the degree of desiccation between A.D. 200 and A.D. 400 was sufficient to have had marked repercussions on the economic, social, and political life of Rome.

Whilst some have tried to prove climatic stability, others have maintained that progressive desiccation has occurred in particular areas. There are many apparent grounds for this contention. Certainly, no one can doubt that some parts of the world receive today less rain than at some earlier phase of their history. Egypt and southern Baluchistan are certainly drier today than they were, for example, in the third millennium B.C.[1] Similarly, as Douglas's careful study of the sequoia trees of California indicated, the climate there is drier today than in the 1st century A.D., and if Huntington's argument is accepted, the same is true of the eastern Mediterranean. Further, it is arguable that Central Asia is drier today than it was, say, in 5000 B.C., but the evidence is very scanty and doubtful. On the other hand, it seems no less certain that some areas have become much wetter than formerly. It is difficult to believe that the remarkable Maya civilisation of Yucatan in Central America could have flourished as it did during the period 100 B.C. to A.D. 350 under conditions of climate and vegetation similar to those of today. Maya ruins occur in many places where tropical heat, rainfall, and jungle prevail today and afford the least healthy and most difficult of the habitats locally available. And finally, the hypothesis of progressive desiccation fails to take account of a whole mass of diverse evidence which suggests pulsations or fluctuations of rainfall throughout historical times.

The idea that the climate of history should be conceived in terms of fluctuations rather than in terms of either stability or progressive desiccation receives support not only from studies of long-period changes in geological times but also from those of short-period variations in the present. The so-called ' 11-year solar cycle,' which has been discovered from the study of actual records of solar radiation, may be, as Huntington suggested, ' the counterpart of the far larger pulsations of the remote past.' Every eleven years, approximately, the radiation of the sun is affected by the appearance of a large number of ' spots ' on its surface. Just what modifications of climate are produced when the sun has many spots is not yet clear. Certainly the greater part of the earth's surface becomes slightly cooler. Moreover, according to Huntington, increased storminess results, and the storm tracks in Europe and North America shift northwards and southwards of their usual courses. It is tempting to suspect, therefore, that if records were available for sufficiently long periods, sunspot cycles occurring at intervals of more than eleven years might be discoverable.

[1] See below, Chapter IX, pp. 138–9.

And if Huntington's contentions are substantiated, it may well be that variations in the spottedness of the sun, howsoever caused, provide a partial explanation of the climatic changes in history.

It is not surprising that historical pulsations of climate have left most traces and proved most important in arid and semi-arid areas where a small variation in rainfall has disproportionate effects on vegetation and thus on animal and human life. It may be useful to indicate here briefly the kinds of evidence which survive in such areas. The former strands of inland seas and lakes, notably the Caspian and Dead Seas, Lop Nor in Central Asia, Lake Mœris in Egypt, Lake Constance, and a number of lakes in California and Arizona, indicate changes in the water level, and may thus reflect climatic changes which can often be dated with some assurance. The stumps of sequoia trees of great age in California and Arizona have been subjected to very careful research which has produced graphs of raininess for a period extending back to two and even three thousand years, for it is a valid assumption that the annual rings of tree growth in dry regions are closely correlated with the rainfall of the few preceding years. Again, archaeological and literary records show how in arid or semi-arid areas civilisations grew and decayed, how cities and trade routes were abandoned, how streams and wells dried up, and how the fauna and flora changed. Finally, there are accounts of unusual climatic conditions—of violent storms and floods and of abnormal seasons—which may indicate not merely the normal aberrations of weather from year to year, but also broad phases of distinctive climate.

It has been claimed by Pettersson and Huntington that the first half of the 14th century provides a remarkably clear instance of the culmination of a period of abnormal climate which prevailed throughout the northern hemisphere. Storms of great violence and destructiveness raged in the North and Baltic seas. The coastlands of England, Holland, Frisia, and Jutland were inundated many times, and changes were effected in the physical and human geography. The Frisian Islands, off the coast of Holland, were reshaped at this time, and the Zuider Zee then assumed its familiar form. In England, villages on the coasts of Holderness and Lincolnshire, and Ravenser Odd, a seaport hard by the Humber, were washed away by high seas. In Europe, winters were often markedly severe, whilst summers were often cool and wet. The great European rivers, including the Thames and the Po, froze over for weeks and even months at a time ; they were subject, too, to exceptional floods, whilst in a few summers they almost dried up. It is believed that in Iceland glaciers extended farther during the first half of the century than they had ever done since the birth of Christ, and Greenland was adversely affected. Frequent failures of harvest in Norway made that country increasingly dependent on grain supplies from the North German Plain, and through their economic repercussions caused much of the political difficulties of the time. The known fact that about the year A.D. 1430 the herrings ceased to spawn

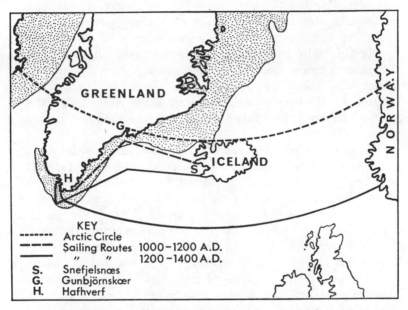

FIG. 22   Medieval sailing routes to Greenland.
*After O. Pettersson.   The stipple
indicates the usual extent of sea ice.*

in the Sound and migrated to the Kattegat may be attributed to the increasing freshness of the water in the Sound, which resulted from contemporary changes in the circulation of the oceans. The open-sea routes between Norway, Iceland, and Greenland, which were well frequented by the Vikings between the 10th and 12th centuries, became obstructed by ice, and by the 14th century had been forced along a more southerly course (Fig. 22). Nor were these abnormalities of climate restricted to Europe. In California unusually high rainfall was characteristic during the 14th century, and in Central Asia, as the high levels of Lop Nor and the Caspian Sea suggest, rainfall was high at least in the early decades of the century. In India, on the other hand, the rain-bearing south-west monsoons were so weak that the country suffered drought and, as a result, famines. In north-west India, too, the Mihran, a mighty river which had long shared with the Indus the task of draining water from the Himalayas, disappeared as an independent stream about the year A.D. 1350[1] (Fig. 63, p. 137). We may add that two possible explanations of the climatic stress of the 14th century have been advanced. Chinese sunspot records, which are admittedly of doubtful scientific value, suggest that sunspots were increasing during the 14th century and reached a maximum about A.D. 1372. And Pettersson, by studying the changing relative positions of the sun and moon, argued that the 'tide-generating force' passed from minimum conditions in A.D. 530 to maximum conditions in A.D. 1434. According to this latter view, increased tidal range in the 14th century increased the circulation of the waters of the oceans and thus increased cyclonic activity.

We may conclude this review of climatic changes in history by relating very briefly the epic story of the Viking settlement of southern Greenland, which provides a well-attested and irrefutable instance of adverse climatic change and its effect on history.[2] It must be admitted that even when it enjoyed a relatively genial climate in the late 10th century, southern Greenland was climatically a marginal area for civilised European life based on food-producing. The name Greenland, which was given to the country by an outlaw from Iceland, Eric the Red, in order to attract immigrants, was something of an advertising slogan. The fact remains, however, that the numerous emigrants from Iceland who settled the coastlands of southern Greenland towards the end of the 10th century were able to support themselves mainly by the pasturing of cattle and sheep in the dales, and at the heads and along the margins of fiords where pasture was then available. The sites of old farms indicate the extent of this bold colonial effort, and the graves of settlers, in soil now frozen throughout the year, contain thick masses of plant roots which must formerly have grown under less severe temperatures than those of today. It seems clear that in the early stages of the settlement the edge of the Greenland

---

[1] Sir John Marshall and others, *Mohenjo-Daro and the Indus Civilization* (1931), vol. i., pp. 5–6.

[2] For a full account of this pioneer settlement and its failure, see Poul Nörlund, *Viking Settlers in Greenland*, trans. W. E. Calvert (1936). On this problem of climatic change, see the reasoned discussion, *loc. cit.*, pp. 145–8.

glaciers stood much farther north than it does today, and that there were open seas between Iceland and the coasts of southern Greenland. The climate began to worsen from about A.D. 1200 onwards ; it became even more severe in the 14th century. The slow decline of the colonies was then accelerated, and in the following century they became extinct. The Eskimoes, who made their livelihood by hunting seals near the edge of the ice, moved southwards during the 14th century and attacked the Viking settlements : their southerly movement indicates that the ice was spreading southwards. It is evident that the Vikings suffered from the adverse effects of increasing cold on the vegetation which undermined their pastoral farming, and also from the weakening of contacts with Iceland and Norway, with which they were politically bound. They were apparently unable to adapt themselves to the Eskimo's way of life, and despite their superior material culture could not defend themselves. The study of the skeletons of the last survivors tells a pitiable story ; the descendants of the hardy Viking pioneers were 'an inactive flock of debilitated individuals, undersized and deformed.'

CHAPTER V

Routes

The road is branded on the soil. It sows seeds of life--houses, hamlets, villages, and towns.

P. VIDAL DE LA BLACHE, *Principles of Human Geography* (1926)

THE study of routes, whether by land, water, or air, forms an important and common interest to the geographer and the historian. For the former they exist as the means of present-day transportation and as features woven into the landscape, the explanation of which is his principal concern. For the latter they are of interest as the essential instruments by which peoples and ideas were diffused, and the activities of commerce, travel, and war were conducted. It is unnecessary to emphasise the fact that the road in its various forms—the hunters' trail, the drovers' road, the mule path, the ridgeway, and the engineered road of Roman and of modern times—has played everywhere throughout history a vital rôle, 'as a sustenance without which organised society would be impossible.'[1] From the standpoint of geography the routes of history raise many problems. How far, if at all, can we postulate the former existence of 'natural routes,' that is, ways which have been marked out by nature as practicable to man and beast? Is there sure ground for the idea that man's earliest roads were the tracks beaten out by wild animals? Should we, in contrast, conceive of routes as solely man-made features sketched upon the soil? Finally, were the ways along which men moved broadly defined by physical geography, or did men themselves in all arbitrariness blaze their own trails?

We may reasonably believe that natural routes existed where, by reason of their physique, vegetation, and climate, particular zones of country lay open and passable. Such possibilities of easy movement were afforded in tracts which were free of dense forests, impeding

[1] Hilaire Belloc, *The Road* (1924), Preface.

marshes, and mountainous obstacles, above all in grasslands and steppes. Rivers also, notwithstanding their individual characters and physical difficulties—drifting tree trunks and ice, changes of level, currents, shoals, freezing, and shifting channels—often provided routes, and means of locomotion too, though only downstream. Similarly, the seas afforded natural routes, when once a sufficient mastery of ship-building and of navigation had been acquired. Again, snow-clad lowlands, as in Russia, offered innumerable routes for travel by sledge, although with the spring thaw wide waterlogged areas obstructed transportation. Finally, the gaps between, and the passes through, mountainous areas presented not only lines of least resistance but often the only practicable ways, prior to the construction of tunnels and the use of aircraft.

In the fauna and flora of different geographical milieus, nature provided the materials with which man learnt to devise means of transport suited to the particular local conditions. The extensive steppe–desert belt of the Old World [1] (Fig. 60, p. 130), where pastoral farming, together with cultivation in favoured parts, prevailed early, was particularly well endowed by nature with domesticable animals, and with flat, dry, and open surfaces appropriate to the use of draught and pack animals. Natural obstacles to overland transport—dense forests, high mountains, and marshes—were minimal in this belt, although stretches of deep and arid sands and the ranges of young fold mountains, as in Central Asia, had to be negotiated. The open spaces of Central Asia have often been likened to a great sea, so easily do they permit passage without necessary change in the means of transport, and the camel and the horse, both native to the region and capable of domestication, became the ships respectively of the desert and the steppe. Both were well equipped physiologically to range over broad, level, and open areas, where the vegetation and water essential for their sustenance were widely scattered. Similarly, in other parts of the world, characterised by different conditions of physique, climate, and vegetation, other native animals were domesticated and adapted, though with varying degrees of efficiency, to the environment. Thus in Egypt and Mesopotamia, as in the Mediterranean lands, the ass was a useful servant, although he could not stand the cold of countries farther north. In the Andean highlands of South America the llama was the only beast of burden, but amongst the natives of North

[1] See below, Chapter IX.

America no baggage animals were employed, since neither the bison nor the caribou was ever domesticated. By acclimatisation, and by selective breeding too, useful animals were introduced into lands beyond, and climatically different from, their original habitats. The horse, above all, proved very adaptable to different climates, and the hybrid mule, which is stronger than the ass and surer-footed than the horse, became the most dependable baggage animal in rough and steeply graded country, and was adaptable to lands which were too cold for the ass.

Many local inventions which, with varying degrees of success, met the needs of transportation in different localities invariably bore ' an environmental stamp.' [1] This is true, for example, of the many forms of river craft known to history and prehistory : boats or rafts were made of inflated ox hides, of bundles of reeds, of hollowed tree trunks, of seal skins, or of birch bark, according to the animal and vegetation products available from place to place. It is true, too, of more fundamental discoveries, such as that of the wheel. As might be expected on geographical grounds, this great discovery was made in a flat lowland where the best conditions obtained for its use in traction. The earliest use of the wheel—it was first made of wood—is attested in the riverine plains of Egypt and Lower Mesopotamia.[2] The wheel was employed also in the steppe-lands of Central Asia, where topographical conditions again facilitated its use, and the great covered horse-drawn wagons, such as those used by the Scythians and later by the Mongols, became a characteristic means of transportation amongst the nomadic folk of Central Asia. For this form of transport, as for that speedier means, horse-riding, nature provided over wide areas, except where deep sands or mountains occurred, broad, firm, and flat roads which were much supe.ior to many of the artificial roads of China. Similarly, as the Romans discovered, a heavy wheeled plough was invented in the plain of northern Gaul, where it was as well suited to the local surface features as it was ill-adaptable to the tiny hilly fields characteristic in the Mediterranean lands.

Let us now attempt to answer our first question. In what senses, if at all, did natural routes exist ? We have seen that in certain areas, especially in Central Asia, geography indicates vast terrains where transportation of men and goods could be undertaken without the need of constructed roads. Further, we may say that geographical

[1] P. Vidal de la Blache, *Principles of Human Geography* (1926), p. 351.
[2] See below, Chapter IX.

conditions—the distribution of land and sea, of relief features, of navigable rivers, and of natural vegetation—define certain broadly zonal routes as the most practicable, though not necessarily the shortest, between separated human habitats. In this sense, therefore, routes, as distinct from roads, can be said to have existed before men marked out their own ways, either by the deliberate building of roads or, as was more common, by the continual tread of their comings and goings between particular objectives.

Among the roads which have grown, in contrast to those which were constructed by Roman legionaries or by modern engineers, are the familiar ' green roads ' or trackways of England. These form coherent patterns on our downlands and our moorlands, and are often related geographically to evidences of man's presence in prehistoric times. The undulating summits and steep escarpments of our chalk plateaux present firm, well-drained surfaces, along which we trace today long-distance routes, which are sometimes minor roads and sometimes mere tracks. What is interesting about these downland ways, as also about moorland ridgeways, is their independence of the lines of villages which lie along the foot of the scarp and dip-slope of the plateaux. It is clear that they are more ancient than the villages, and that they arose to serve the needs of peoples for whom the uplands rather than the valleys formed the setting to their activities. Certainly, our downland trackways form a remarkable network. The old trackways of the North and South Downs converge on the Hampshire Downs, and continue into Salisbury Plain. From this focus similar tracks led south-westwards across the Dorset Downs to reach the sea at three points, and northwards, by way of the Wiltshire and Marlborough Downs, to the Chiltern plateau, whence one continued to the Norfolk shore of the Wash. Further, distributed alongside these trackways can be found numerous signs of ancient occupation, such as earthworks and contour camps, and barrows or prehistoric graves. It is clear that if we could discover when these camps and graves were first constructed—and on these matters ' field archaeology ' has shed much light—we should be able to determine the antiquity of these routes. Actually, although many sites await excavation, it is probable that our familiar downland earthworks or ' camps ' were completed in the Early Iron Age, say about 500 B.C., although some of them may well have been partially occupied, as was Maiden Castle,[1] by Neolithic

---

[1] See below, Chapter VI, pp. 85 and 87

stock-raisers as early as 2000 B.C. There is reason to believe that some at least of the downland trackways may be as old as this, for evidences derived from barrows, stone circles, pit sites, and flint mines indicate that the downs were occupied from Neolithic times onwards—that is, from about 2000 B.C. Thus it may well be that the Pilgrims Way of the North Downs and the Icknield Way (Fig. 37, p. 84) were stamped out and utilised in the Bronze, and perhaps even in the Neolithic Age, although these roads as they appear today are made up of stretches which have been made or remade at many subsequent periods.

The Pilgrims Way led westwards from the Kentish ports to Salisbury Plain, and it may have linked up with old roads which led as far west as Cornwall, important in prehistoric times as a source of tin. The Icknield Way led from the Wash, one of the chief gateways of eastern England, along the escarpment of the chalk, south-westwards, by way of the Chilterns, and across the upper Thames to Avebury, a prehistoric focus of many downland routes. The Icknield Way is of interest, too, as an illustration of how old roads become permanent geographical factors and exert an influence on historical events. Thus it is believed that the West Saxons, whose settlement in the Hampshire Basin formed the nucleus of the kingdom of Wessex, entered England by way of the Wash, and moved south-westwards along the Icknield Way. So also the existence of the Icknield Way helps to explain the siting of a number of towns (see Fig. 37).

What was the origin of these ancient trackways? It is certainly relevant to note that they occur in country which, owing to its vegetation cover, its porous subsoil, and its natural drainage, offered to prehistoric intruders the easiest means of livelihood and of inter-communication. Except where deposits of clay and brick-earth over-lie the chalk, the downlands possessed a vegetation cover of grass interspersed with beech and ash, for the thin soils and the porous subsoils proved inimical to large trees and heavy undergrowth. Together with stretches of sandy and gravelly country, and the gravel-floored terraces of rivers, the downlands were attractive, as the marshes and forested clay-lands were repellent, to peoples ill-equipped to undertake the stern tasks of clearing forest and draining marshes. It is easy to see why, therefore, as distribution maps of prehistoric cultures indicate,[1] peoples continually occupied the downlands, which could be reached directly from the sea in Dorset, in Sussex, and in

[1] See Sir Cyril Fox, *The Personality of Britain*, published by the National Museum of Wales, Cardiff, 4th ed., 1959.

Kent, and found there pasture for their flocks and herds and conditions suitable for primitive agriculture. But were the actual trackways marked out by man, or were they already visible on the ground as a result of the movements of wild animals ?

The belief that the routes first used by man in Europe and North America were the tracks impressed by wild animals in the course of their movements in search of water and of pasture has been expounded and elaborated by many writers, including Thorold Rogers. They have described how in England, for example, paths leading from hilltops down to drinking-places or to fords were initially defined by hoofed animals, and how in the North American prairies alleged buffalo trails indicated paths which were utilised in turn by native Indians, American pioneers, and even by railway engineers. To the buffalo (or bison) in particular certain early travellers ascribed not only a considerable sagacity, which enabled it to discover fords and the most easily graded valleys, but also remarkable migratory habits. Actually, many arguments cast doubt on the theory that the human highway originated in the animals' track. It is common knowledge that in level, open country animals spread out widely and do not pursue definite tracks. In Alberta, where the buffalo disappeared about 1882, there were no signs in 1894 of the kind of tracks usually ascribed to it, and no reason to believe that they had been obliterated by man.[1] Many, if not all, of the wild animals of sufficient size to impress a useful track upon the ground were capable swimmers which had no need to seek the fords of rivers : buffaloes were certainly good swimmers, and even domestic cattle, we are told, used to swim across the Menai Strait from Anglesey. Then again, it has been argued that the so-called migrations of buffaloes meant little more than their seeking shelter in woods and scrublands in the dead of winter, and further, that the buffalo was, in fact, one of the most aimless, unreliable, and incalculable wanderers on the face of the earth. In contrast, to cite another recent writer,[2] we are told :

> The herds migrated slowly ; they did not range widely, and their movements were very persistent ; extremely hardy, they could easily weather blizzards which would kill domestic cattle. Keeping closer in the lee of the mountains in winter, the same herds moved along the same routes from one natural pasture to another, until they trod out great lanes of habitual migration.

[1] See on this problem, F. G. Roe, 'The "Wild Animal" Path Origin of Ancient Roads,' *Antiquity*, III (1929), pp. 299–311.

[2] C. Daryll Forde, *Habitat, Economy, and Society* (1934), p. 56.

Whatever may be the correct view of the alleged buffalo trails and their bearing on the development of the routeways of North America, it is not easy to believe that the earliest tracks in England were marked out by cattle. If our downland trackways are conceived as cattle tracks, it would be true to say of many of them that they 'lead from nowhere to nowhere.' If, on the other hand, we regard them as man-made, they can be rationally explained, since they are related to, and linked up, areas of prehistoric settlement, and they have often as their terminals convenient landing-places along our shores.

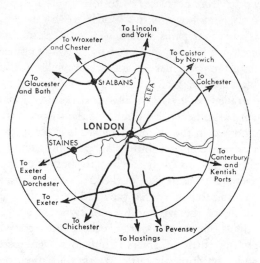

FIG. 23   London as a route focus in Roman times.

It is remarkable how the present English landscape presents a variegated pattern of roads which has been woven in the course of its long history, and this pattern, like that presented by the outcrops of the rocks, can be analysed into distinguishable and datable elements.[1] Each of the major phases of the history and prehistory of England had its characteristic routes, which were either designed, or grew up, to serve the needs of the time, and each successive phase inherited a system of routes to which it added its own. We have already suggested that some of our moorland and downland trackways, which lie along the ridges or hillsides, were marked out by the passage of prehistoric folk,

[1] See H. J. Randall, *History in the Open Air* (1936), chap. ii, for expert guidance about prehistoric English roads.

who found a home in the more open parts of these uplands long before our present towns and villages were founded. During the first few centuries A.D., southern Britain received for the first time an arterial system of highways, focused on London, itself a newcomer on the scene. These Roman roads, which were efficiently engineered, were printed almost indelibly on the face of the country, and long continued in use. To our Anglo-Saxon and Scandinavian forbears, who certainly made use of pre-existing roads in the course of their settlement, we may attribute some at least of the many winding country lanes—the

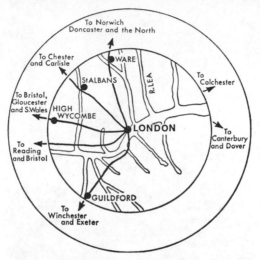

FIG. 24   London as a route focus in the 14th century.
*According to the Gough map, which did not mark
all the contemporary routes convergent on London.*

roads which 'twist and squirm'—which linked up fields, farms, villages, and market towns. If these colonising folk have left little record of their local routes, we know that they settled intensively in lowlands and river valleys, which had been formerly much avoided. And the type of road of which they made most use in their everyday life was doubtless not the military highway left by the Romans but local lanes, such as those which G. K. Chesterton had in mind when he wrote : ' The rolling English drunkard made the rolling English road.' Again, in early 14th century, as a contemporary map, known as the Gough map, shows, a system of routes existed which coincided in part with the alignments of Roman roads, but introduced also new alignments which were related to the needs of the time.[1] Thus although London clearly remained the chief focus of routes (Figs. 23, 24, and 25), there were roads independent of London, such as that which, by way of Oxford, connected the two Hamptons—Northampton and Southampton. We could continue this brief review of 'period route patterns' by examining the 17th-century road system, as it was mapped by John Ogilby in his *Britannia* in 1675, the engineered roads and railways which were constructed in the 19th century, and finally, the motor roads of today. It need hardly be emphasised that

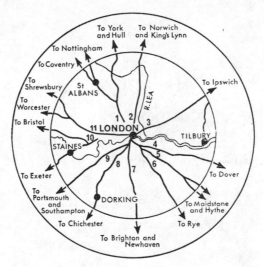

FIG. 25   London as a route focus in the 17th century.
Some of these roads—e.g. 2, 3, and 4—broadly coincided with the lines of Roman roads.   cp. Fig. 23.

knowledge of the routes existing at particular periods is historically important in relation to the problems of transportation, travel, trade, and war.

Let us by way of illustration examine in two particular cases the natural setting of routes. We will explore first the natural routes along which civilised ways of life first penetrated continental Europe, and second some of the historical routes of England and, more particularly, of Wales.

[1] See F. M. Stenton, 'The Road System of Medieval England,' *Economic History Review*, vol. vii (1936), No. 1, pp. 1–21.

Neolithic culture, when it appeared belatedly and for the first time in continental Europe in the third millennium B.C., represented a level of knowledge and technical accomplishment which may fitly be termed civilised. European folk who had reached the Neolithic stage of culture were no longer mere food collectors but food producers : they engaged in agriculture and animal husbandry. Further, although Neolithic civilisation in continental Europe displayed original and individual features in different areas, it seems right to explain its initial rise in terms of stimuli which came from outside : by the intrusion of peoples and ideas from earlier centres of civilisation. These centres

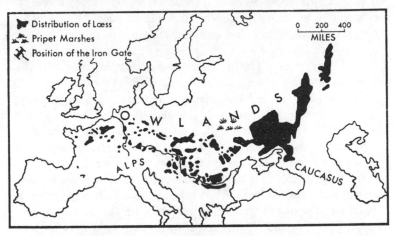

FIG. 26   The distribution of loess in Europe.

were primarily Egypt, Mesopotamia, Asia Minor, Crete, and other parts of the Ægean world.[1]

We must conceive of Europe in the third millennium, when Neolithic culture spread slowly westwards, as widely covered with dense forests and undergrowth, except where tree growth was precluded by high altitude, bad drainage, or exposure to strong winds. The climate of Europe during the Neolithic period was wet and warm at first (Atlantic phase) and later during the sub-boreal phase, became cooler but not so dry as was earlier believed. It used to be thought that the sub-boreal climate proved inimical to tree growth on soils which overlay loess (see Fig. 26) and on those over limestone rocks,

[1] See below, Chapter IX.

as also on sands and gravels, and that such areas presented steppe-heath flora easily occupied by Neolithic colonists. However, it is now argued that Neolithic intruders, whose economy combined primitive cultivation with pastoral farming, pressed into wooded areas, especially those of light textured soil and porous subsoil, using fire and axes of flint and stone to clear woodlands for settlement. Such settled farm lands, commonly on plateau or valley-gravel sites, became lands of relatively easy movement. Moreover, they provided soils which, given the rudimentary technique of the time, were the best suited to cultivation.

Thus major route-ways of Neolithic Europe sought the dry, forest-cleared or naturally open country and avoided the obstructions set by mountains, forests, and marshes. We should conceive of these routes as broad zones, except where narrow gaps and mountain passes canalised movement. The distribution of archaeological finds which can be assigned to this period is concordant with this view.

One major route led diagonally across Europe from its steppe margin in the south-east towards southern Belgium, by way of the Galician platform and a foothill zone which lies below the central mountain system of Europe and the North European Plain (Fig. 27). It was defined to some extent by the spread of loess deposits (Fig. 26) and it outflanked not only the mountainous zone but also the extensive marshes of the river Pripet. At its south-eastern end, this route made contact by way of the Ural–Caspian Gate with the broad steppes of Central Asia ; so also it was linked with south-west Asia by routes which skirted or crossed the Caucasus mountains. From the northern shores of the Black Sea alternative routes lay open towards the west. One led into the Wallachian Plain and the Bulgarian Plateau, which lie respectively to the north and south of the lower Danube, and another, by means of passes across the Carpathians, gave access to the upland Basin of Transylvania. From Transylvania it was easy to move down into the Hungarian Plain ; Hungary could also be reached from the diagonal route, by way of the Moravian Gate, which is confined between the Sudetes and Beskid mountains (Fig. 28, p. 69).

Other long-distance routes were afforded by the river Danube (see Fig. 26). The lower Danube was doubtless navigable then, as it is today, but insurmountable physical difficulties must have been met at and just above the Iron Gate cataract, owing to the swift current of the river as it sweeps through narrow, winding, and rocky gorges. The Hungarian Plain, which lies astride the middle Danube, could be

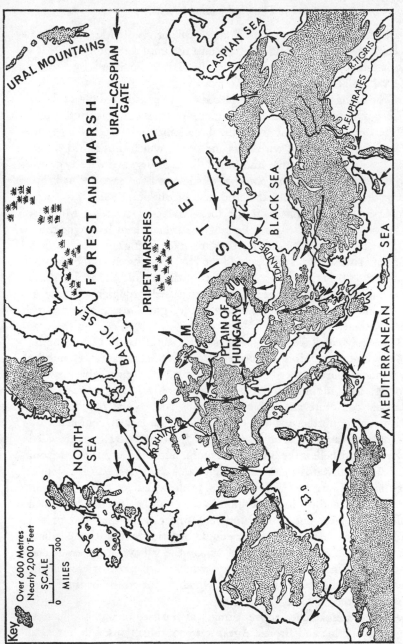

KEY

Over 600 Metres
Nearly 2,000 Feet

SCALE
0   300
MILES

URAL MOUNTAINS

URAL–CASPIAN
GATE

FOREST AND MARSH

S T E P P E

PRIPET MARSHES

BALTIC SEA

NORTH
SEA

CASPIAN SEA

R. TIGRIS

R. EUPHRATES

BLACK SEA

R. DANUBE

PLAIN OF HUNGARY

M

R. RHINE

MEDITERRANEAN SEA

FIG. 27 Zones of access into prehistoric Europe.
M marks the position of the Moravian Gate.

reached, as we have seen, from Transylvania or via the Moravian Gate. A third route, which did not come into use until the Bronze Age, led from the Ægean northwards across the Balkan Peninsula by way of the valleys of the Vardar and Morava rivers.

The Hungarian Plain was so placed and so constituted physically as to become a great route focus and centre of Neolithic civilisation. Wide open areas, aloof from the broad marshes which fringe the Danube, were covered with loess and sands, which thus afforded easy passage as well as pasture and arable land. We have already noted how access into Hungary could be made from the east, and it is not surprising geographically that the first Neolithic peasants of central Europe were established on the loess-covered plateau of Moravia, whence they penetrated into the Hungarian Plain near by. One route ran westwards and another northwards from Hungary, along which the new civilised ways of life could spread. One passed up the Danube valley into Bavaria, whence the plains of the middle Rhine, in Alsace and Baden, could be reached. The other passed through the Moravian Gate, and thence westwards along the diagonal route towards the lower Rhine.

We may conclude our survey of the natural routes of Europe by noting that entry into the continent from its Mediterranean peninsulas was practicable at only a few selected points. It is remarkable how the young, fold mountains of the Pyrenees, Alps, Dinaric Alps, and Balkans constitute an almost continuous rim to the Mediterranean Basin on its northern side. Passage northwards was confined to a number of gates, gaps, or passes (Fig. 27). The water gate provided by the Dardanelles, the Sea of Marmora, and the Bosporus led from the Ægean towards the Danube delta and the south Russian steppe. Farther west was the Vardar–Morava route which led to Belgrade on the Danube, and the low but difficult passes of the eastern Alps which afforded a short cut to the middle Danube from the head of the Adriatic Sea. Ingress into France could be made up the Rhône valley, or by the isthmian route marked out by the valleys of the Aude and Garonne. Finally, there were ways which outflanked or crossed the Pyrenees, as there were high passes which in the course of time were opened in the Alps.

The routes sketched above, along which passed civilising influences in the Neolithic and Bronze Ages, were continually used in historical times. From Central Asia successive waves of nomadic horsemen swept through the Ural–Caspian Gate, whence they moved west along one or more routes, either to ravage, as did the Huns ; to conquer, as did the Mongols ; or to settle down, as did the Magyars and Bulgars.

Increasingly, as they advanced in material culture, peoples marked out and improved roads to serve their changing needs. It is remarkable how closely these were usually adapted to ' the lie of the land ' and to the lines of least resistance. Although we must not erroneously ascribe to folk of prehistoric and early historical times the relatively full

FIG. 28   The Moravian Gate and its approaches.

knowledge of country which we now possess, it is clear that many of them, like our own Anglo-Saxon ancestors, had an eye for country, a sort of geographical horse-sense, characteristic perhaps of those who live closely bound to the soil. It is true that today roads can be built without too much regard to physical circumstances, but it is equally clear that such regardlessness may result in high constructional costs. In historical times only exceptionally were routes aligned arbitrarily, as was the St Petersburg–Moscow railway. In this case the nature of the Russian Plain facilitated the whim of the Tsar—the construction of

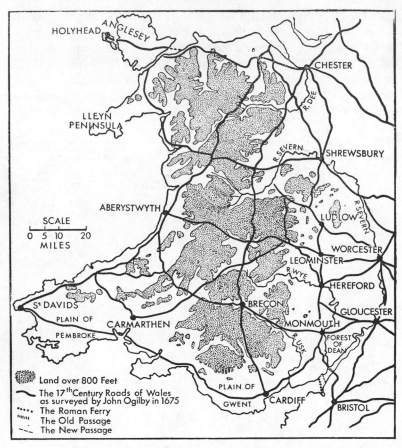

FIG. 29   Wales and the Border : 17th-century roads.

The roads are from the Ordnance Survey map of 17th-century England and Wales, with the sanction of the Director-General.

a railroad along the straight line which joins those two towns. In more physically variegated country, however, such geometric alignments of routes were not easily attainable. The Roman roads appear to show a fine disregard of local features of relief and elevation, but actually they often sought the easiest lines, as they avoided low, floodable lands. The Roman roads across the high Pennine moorlands of England, as indeed those of later periods, made good use of the easier gradients afforded by river valleys and of 'saddles' which avoided the broader and more elevated parts of the chain. Only later

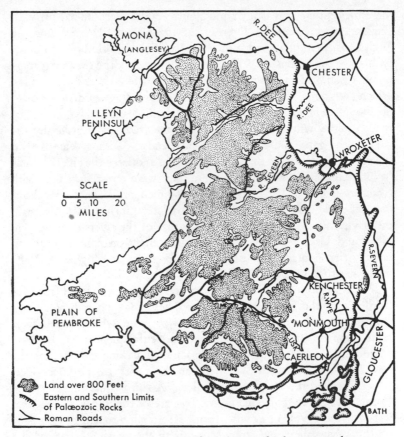

FIG. 30   Wales and the Border : limits of Palaeozoic rocks
and Roman roads.

*The roads are from the Ordnance Survey map of Roman
Britain, with the sanction of the Director General.*

did route-makers attain such a mastery over this physical environment
that they could carry canals, in tunnels, from one flank of the Pennines
to the other, and it is unnecessary to insist that railways, there as
elsewhere, normally followed the easiest gradients.

A brief review of the roads which led into Wales from the Border
will serve to illustrate the contention that routes were usually well
adapted to the conditions of relief.   All but the more hardy and
venturesome travellers were long repelled by the wild, barren, and
lonely uplands of Wales, and it was not until the last two decades of

the 18th century that North and South Wales were linked up with England by stage coach. Even in the 1720s Daniel Defoe found the Welsh roads fatiguing and somewhat frightening, although—in comparing the mountains of Wales, which are merely the surviving fragments of an ancient mountain system, with the Alps and the Andes, which are young 'fold mountains' in an active stage of denudation— he indulged in geographical licence. Almost inevitably the major roads sought, where they could, the easier gradients afforded by the valleys, the gaps, and the marginal lowlands. Within Wales it was the plateau levels rather than the moors which offered the chief obstacle to internal communications, because they were covered in part with treacherous bogs. Fig. 29 shows how much of Wales stood above 800 feet, and how little was relatively lowland. It shows also the main easterly trend of the drainage, notably that of the rivers Dee, Severn, Wye, and Usk, which had an important effect on communications, namely that contact between lowland England and highland Wales was easier than between the different parts of Wales.

We may distinguish some six 'natural routes' which led from the Border into the interior of Wales. These may be indicated conveniently in relation to the Border towns from which travellers or armies started their journey during and subsequently to the later Middle Ages. Two routes led from Chester, passing either along the low, hilly strip of north Wales, or up the valley of the upper Dee, which is called the Vale of Llangollen. A third route can be traced from either Shrewsbury or Ludlow by way of the upper Severn, that is, through the Vale of Powis. From Hereford, a fourth route passed up the Wye valley, and from Monmouth the upper Usk afforded a fifth route, which continued, by way of the Towy valley, to Carmarthen. Finally, from Gloucester the way lay open westwards through the lowland which flanks the Severn estuary, and thence through the coastal lowlands of Monmouth and Glamorgan. An alternative entry into South Wales could be made by using the ferry across the tidal waters of the Severn estuary (see Fig. 29).

Fig. 30 shows the known stretches of Roman roads in Wales, which remained in use throughout the Middle Ages as routes for armies and for colonists from England. It is striking that these roads were much less straight than those of lowland England. In outflanking the many obstacles presented by the physique of Wales, they deviated along the lines of least resistance. Reference to Fig. 30 shows that the natural routes enumerated above were represented in almost every case by

Roman roads. It should be noted that the Roman roads in Wales tended to avoid the wet and wooded valley bottoms in preference to the dry slopes of the valley. The starting-points for a journey into Wales in Roman times were, in the case of Chester and Gloucester, the same as in later times, but the Roman prototypes of Shrewsbury and Hereford were respectively Wroxeter and Kenchester. Finally, it should not be inferred that Wales lacked local routes, as distinct from the main highways which led towards the Border. In the course of their seasonal movement of cattle up to high pastures, as in their driving of cattle to market towns, the Welsh made use of numerous ridgeways and other upland tracks. Thus until the end of the 18th century the traditional routes in the Glamorganshire plateau followed the ridges between the deep, narrow valleys which were entrenched within it. It was only with the development of the coal resources of the area that these valleys were cleared of their woods, drained, and settled, and that roads, canals, or railways were aligned along them.[1]

[1] On the early roads of South Wales much light is shed by Dr W. Rees's *Handbook and Maps of South Wales and the Border in the 14th Century* (1933). For an account of the ridgeways of Wales during the Dark Ages, see the papers on Offa's Dyke, by Sir Cyril Fox and D. W. Phillips, in *Archæologia Cambrensis*, 1926–31.

CHAPTER VI

Towns

Man organizes the site prepared by Nature, so as to enable her to satisfy his needs and desires.

P. VIDAL DE LA BLACHE

THE striking discoveries of archaeologists in Egypt, Mesopotamia, and north-west India have revealed clearly not only the great antiquity of urban settlement but also its remarkable rôle in the development of civilisation. City life provided the social milieu in which human culture reached its most original and developed forms, so much so, that it is not surprising that the words 'civilisation' and 'city' are derived from a common root. The earliest known towns arose within the riverine lands of the lower Nile, the lower Euphrates and Tigris, and the Indus rivers about, or soon after, 3000 B.C. Their appearance then, as a new form of settlement distinct from the village, has been rightly acclaimed one of the chief and novel features of a great cultural revolution. According to Gordon Childe,[1] there were only three major cultural revolutions throughout the whole length of human history, of which two occurred in the riverine lands between 6000 and 3000 B.C. during a phase of so-called Neolithic culture.[2] The first revolution, which took place in the 5th millennium, was characterised by the discovery of agriculture, of the domestication of animals, and of many useful arts, such as weaving, by groups of people who dwelt in villages. The second revolution, in the 3rd millennium, brought with it the town, together with many inventions and new practices, such as metallurgy, architecture in brick and stone, trade, writing, and the use of a calendar. On this arresting view of the origin and development of civilised life, only the Industrial Revolution of the 18th, 19th, and 20th centuries A.D. remained drastically to modify the material basis of civilisation.

---

[1] V. G. Childe, *Man Makes Himself* (1936).
[2] See below, Chapter IX.

The rise of towns, throughout the Old World at least, may be explained as the result of the diffusion of the idea and forms of city life from the three areas of primary or earliest civilisation which we have noted above. It is difficult, however, to accept the extreme diffusionist view that discoveries and inventions were made in, and diffused from, one place, such as Egypt, for in Central America, when Columbus arrived there, the urban type of settlement had emerged, independently, it would seem, of contacts with the Old World. It seems reasonable to believe that the flow of cultural currents from either Egypt or Mesopotamia explains the rise of cities in Crete, Asia Minor, Syria, and Palestine. It fell later to the Phœnician cities along the Syrian coast and to the cities of Greece, which had received stimuli from Crete near by, to establish numerous cities along the coastlands of the Mediterranean and Black Sea Basins, whilst in Tuscany and even beyond the Apennines the Etruscans established inland and coastal cities. The Roman Empire, as it grew, founded cities beyond the limits of the Mediterranean lands, as far west as southern Britain, and as far east and north as the valleys of the Rhine and Danube. The sites of many Roman towns bear towns to this day, but in some cases the post-Roman towns occupy sites near to, though not identical with, the Roman site, as in the case of St Albans which grew up close to the former Roman Verulamium. Nor is it always clear that cities found on or near Roman sites had a continuous history. In the course of the Middle Ages, too, both beyond the Rhine and Danube, as also within the area formerly ruled by Rome, many new towns were founded.

Since they are such complex entities and present so many facets, towns can be classified in various ways. When we speak of market towns, seaports, capital cities, county towns, or industrial towns, we are distinguishing them in terms of their varied functions. Alternatively, we may classify them according to the size of their population. Again, towns differ in their legal status and may be classified on this basis. But however we distinguish them, towns usually present recognisable features on the ground unlike those of rural settlements. A relatively large aggregation of population on a particular site, a town is engaged in specialised functions, such as trade, industry, defence, administration, political or ecclesiastical organisation, and these are reflected in its markets, workshops, harbours, courts of law, fortifications, and cathedrals. These functions were commonly, if not exclusively, urban ; agriculture, on the other hand, was usually though not exclusively, associated with rural types of settlement—

villages, hamlets, and homesteads. Finally, a normal geographical feature of a town is its ' nodality ' : in general, a town tends to become a focus of routes which permit wide regional or even international relationships. This superiority over the village in facility of communication and transport is the result of human effort, but it is remarkable how often the geographical site and setting of towns are such as to imply a natural convergence of routes.

Our problem here is : In what ways does geography throw light on the history of towns ? The answer can be stated briefly. By studying towns as particular elements of the countryside the geographer can explain, above all, the physical site and the positional setting of towns, and in so doing he is able to supply useful clues not only to their origin and distribution, but also to their functions and their changing fortunes.

Close study of particular towns suggest that their sites, far from being fortuitous, appear to have been rationally selected. ' Man chooses and then utilises the site prepared by nature.' Admittedly, his needs and purposes continually change. Sometimes, indeed often, the primary need was for a naturally defensible site, protected by marshes or waters or by the form of the land. At other times settlers, such as the Greek colonists of antiquity, sought rather the means of agriculture, although they sought also facilities for defence and maritime trade. Sometimes the purpose of the foundation was political : thus in the case of Washington a federal capital was required in such a position that it could be reached conveniently by deputies from all of the thirteen constituent states. But whether towns were founded deliberately as towns, as in the case of Roman London, or whether they grew spontaneously from humble beginnings, as did Paris and Rome, the factor of site seems to have been important. In the formation of towns two elements may be detected. First, there is the human group, which may establish a castle, an abbey, a market, or a port ; and second, there is the physical element, the site, which, if well chosen from the standpoints of local and regional advantages, may foster the survival and growth of the town.

The advantages of particular sites were sometimes rather latent than recognised by those who first occupied them. The Greek emigrants from the Chalcidice peninsula, because they settled at Chalcedon rather than at Byzantium, which lay just across the Bosporus strait, were accused of ' blindness.' Actually, they were farmers, not traders or fishermen, and found in the vicinity of Chalcedon excellent lands well suited to their agricultural experience. The Greeks from Megara, who made the first settlement at Byzantium (Constantinople) *c.* 657 B.C., did not at first appreciate the great potentialities of this incomparable site, for they, too, were primarily farmers. It was only later, when they had found agriculture difficult, owing to attacks from the landward side, that they turned their attention to the rich fish resources of the Golden Horn and to the profits of the Black Sea–Ægean trade.

It is clear, too, that some settlements, which were intended by their founders to become towns, failed to develop because they occupied unfavourable sites and positions. This was the fate of some of the less carefully chosen foundations of King Edward I. It is important to remember, too, that towns, like organisms, undergo a process of natural selection. Present-day towns include those which have proved fittest to survive, and in what constitutes survival value the geographical factors of site and position have certainly a place.

Some at least of the activities of towns appear to have been suggested or fostered by the physical character of their sites and their wider geographical settings. The position of a town in relation to local mineral deposits, to agricultural possibilities, and to the facilities for communication and transport by land or by water, may throw some light on its importance and its economic activities.

Again, geographical study suggests an important generalisation about the distribution of certain towns and also a reason for their existence. Towns are commonly aligned along the junction of physically contrasted zones. It is tempting to infer that the *raison d'être* of such towns is implied in this geographical fact. For it seems probable that, once people become sufficiently organised, the need arises for points conveniently placed for the exchange of the contrasted and complementary products of the contiguous environments, as also for the change in the means of transport to which each is suited. Thus the most obvious illustration of such a zone of differentiation is the coastland, where a change in the means of transport becomes necessary from the seagoing ship to transport by land or by river craft, and whither the products of the land may be brought, together with those of the sea (fish, etc.) and those from oversea. Similarly, at the junction of mountain and plain, or at the junction of the steppe and the 'sown,' towns may, according to this view, be expected to arise.

Some writers have argued, not very convincingly, that urban development is particularly marked in certain climatic zones. In so far as climate may be an explanatory factor in the distribution of towns, its influence can have been only indirect, and would have to be sought through its effect on vegetation and thus on the means of livelihood.

We have suggested above that in some cases at least changing physical factors may affect the fortunes of a town. Many seaports have been cut off from effective access to the sea by deposits of silt of marine or fluvial origin, or by the formation of shingle beaches, as a result of which their waterway approaches have been blocked or

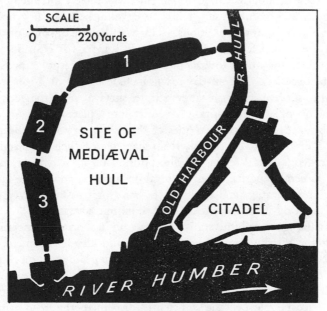

FIG. 31 The port of Hull, *c.* A.D. 1830.
*The docks marked 1, 2, and 3 were constructed between 1778
and 1829 along the line of the medieval walls and ditches.*

shallowed. In some cases cities were submerged by tidal waters, or by river floods, or by volcanic eruptions ; occasionally, too, towns have disappeared as a result of coast erosion. Changes in the fortunes of towns resulted also from economic or political changes in their markets at home or abroad. In such cases the significant factor was geographical only in a secondary sense ; it was not related directly to physical conditions but rather to the changed uses to which these were put.

Let us now attempt by examining some 'specimen towns' to justify and illustrate this general discussion.

We have suggested that the sites of towns were not selected haphazardly but represent a more or less rational choice from the possibilities available in any area. Apparent or real exceptions to this rule can certainly be discovered. There are some towns which were placed as it were in sheer defiance of geographical conditions. Le Havre was built in the middle of the 17th century amidst the marshes of the Seine estuary ; Yokohama persists on a site subject to

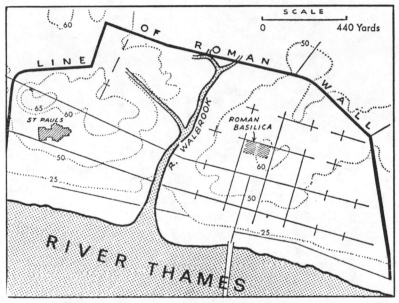

FIG. 32   The site of London.

Approximate contours are shown in feet: after H. Ormsby, ' London on the Thames,'
map XIV. The Roman roads and bridge are shown, but their breadth is not true to the scale.

periodical earthquakes ; Kairuan (=' the tent ') was founded by the Arabs as their capital of Tunisia, in the 7th century A.D., for good strategical reasons, yet in the midst of an area of arid steppe ; and of Milan it has been argued that almost any site near by would have served equally well as a focus on the plain of Lombardy for routes from the passes of the Central Alps. Perhaps it is wisest to argue that in most cases the physical site chosen offered advantages and disadvantages, with the former usually predominant. Thus the town of Hull, the natural haven of which well equipped it to serve as a medieval seaport, lacked adequate supplies of drinking water and stood

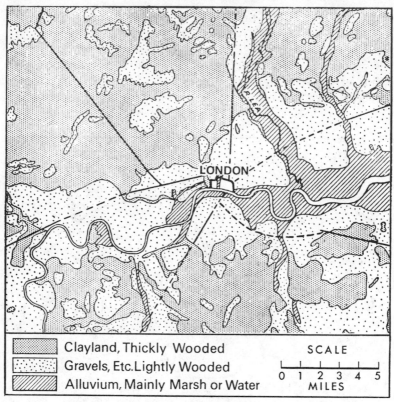

Fig. 33   Roman London in its geographical setting.
After R. M. Wheeler, modified.   Roman roads are shown.

on low ' salty soil ' which was liable to occasional flooding by the tidal
Humber (Fig. 31).

Among seaports we can distinguish several typical sites.   One of
the commonest found in Britain, as in other tidal coastlands, is the
bridge-port site near the head of river estuaries.   Many of our great
seaports, past and present, notably London, Bristol, and Chester,
conform to this type ; so do also a large number of more local
importance, such as Colchester, Warrington, Preston, and Bridgwater.

London, which appears for the first time as a Roman foundation in
the 1st century A.D., occupied two gravel-capped hills divided by the
river Walbrook, and stood near the tapering head of the Thames
estuary, where bridge-building first became practicable (Figs. 32
and 33).   Below London one may search in vain for a comparable site,

which afforded at the same time security against flood and attack and permitted the building of a bridge. Down-stream from London the estuary is flanked almost everywhere by alluvial flats which were subject to inundation at high water of spring tides. Where hard rock actually occurs on the banks of the river, as at Greenwich and Purfleet, there is no similar 'dry point' on the other bank; moreover, the breadth of the river made bridging there an almost impossible task in

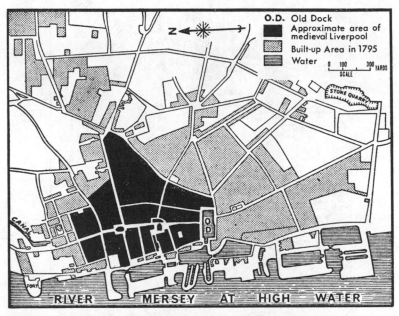

FIG. 34 Liverpool in A.D. 1795.
The Old Dock occupied the position of the Pool.

ancient times. The tides served to carry ships upstream to London, as the ebb waters helped to carry them seawards. Water supply, too, was available on the site of London from small streams, now covered in: these issued from the base of the gravel deposits which overlie hills of impervious London Clay.

Chester and Bristol present essentially analogous site features, together with local differences. The small sandstone plateau upon which medieval Bristol arose was washed on one side by the tidal waters of the Avon, and on two sides by a tributary stream, the Frome; only on one side was it unprotected by water, and on this side was

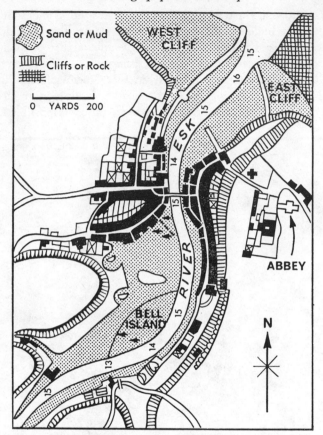

FIG. 35 The town and port of Whitby, Yorks,
in A.D. 1740.

*The figures indicate depths of water, in feet, at high-
water spring tides, and the arrow-heads mark moorings.*

built the medieval castle. Since the Bristol Channel experiences a high
tidal range, there was ample water, though only at high tide, for ships
to approach or leave the town. Further, a little above Bristol, owing
to a change in the gradient of the river bed, the Avon ceased to be
navigable, and this physical fact may have helped to confirm the choice
of the site. Finally Chester, which, like London, had a Roman origin
—it was one of three ' castra ' or fortresses—stood at the head of the
Dee estuary on a hill site.

Another common type of seaport site is that represented by the still flourishing ports of Kingston-upon-Hull and Liverpool. The former, which appeared as a town subsequently to the Domesday Survey (1086) and received its charter from King Edward I, stood at the mouth of a small river which drained into the wide and stormy Humber estuary (Fig. 31). The mouth of the Hull provided shelter and sufficient space for small shipping until the late 18th century; moreover, there was a more than ample depth of water up the Humber

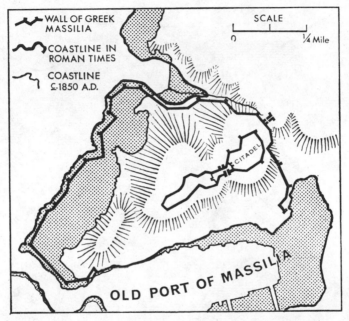

FIG. 36   The site of Massilia (Marseilles) in ancient times.
After Desjardins, simplified.

to Hull, for the deep-water channel actually reached the shore at the site of Hull itself. Liverpool, too, which received a charter from King John and is marked on the famous Gough map, c. 1350,[1] occupied a similar site, but its importance is historically much more recent than that of Hull. Liverpool stood at the mouth of the small river, the Lever, which provided a sheltered tidal haven, called ' The Pool,' and gave access to the broad mouth of the Mersey (Fig. 34). Unlike Hull, it enjoyed the advantage of a high, dry site, afforded by a small plateau

[1] See above, Chapter V, pp. 63-4.

of sandstone. It was a favourable physical factor in the growth of Liverpool as a port that the Mersey estuary narrows below the town, and has as a result a considerable tidal scour and thus deep water. Both at Hull and at Liverpool the construction of docks to accommodate their rapidly growing trade became necessary in the 18th century.

We may note briefly two other types of port sites, which may be illustrated by the small yet once active seaport of Whitby and by the

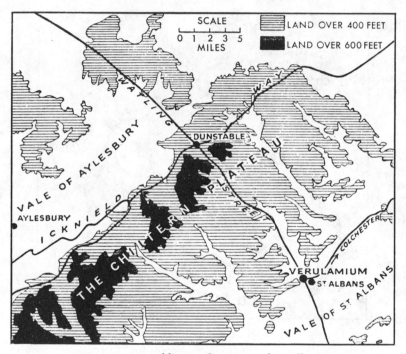

FIG. 37   Dunstable, Verulamium, and St Albans.

historic port of Marseilles (Figs. 35 and 36). Whitby lay at the mouth of a small tidal river (the Esk) on a stretch of inhospitable coast, which was lacking in natural havens. It was important both for its ship-building and as a port of refuge : it found its easiest routeways on the open sea, since it was shut in landwards by high barren moors. Massilia (Marseilles), which was founded as early as about 650 B.C. by Greek colonists, represented a port site commonly found in the non-tidal Mediterranean. Essentially it consisted of a steeply-sided penin-sula, below which lay a small sheltered basin, deep and big enough for

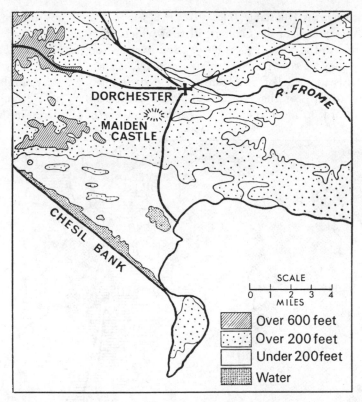

Fɪɢ. 38   Dorchester and Maiden Castle.
*Roman roads are shown.   The ridgeway
shown had a pre-Roman existence.*

the shipping of earlier times, though, as a result of silting, it became useless in modern days, and artificial docks had to be constructed.   It is worth adding that Marseilles, like many of the other chief Mediterranean seaports, stands at a little distance from the mouth of a great river (the Rhône), since, owing to the absence of tides, the rivers build up great marshy deltas.   Moreover, it stands to the eastwards of the Rhône delta, the alluvium of which is carried to the westwards by the anti-clockwise currents characteristic of the Mediterranean Sea.

There is a 'site geography' of inland no less than of maritime cities.   A group of towns well represented in the scarp-lands of southern England and in the Central Valley of Scotland occupies sites either within or hard by gap-ways through plateau areas.   Illustrative of such towns is Dunstable (Fig. 37). It lies in a ' wind gap ' through the escarpment of the Chiltern Plateau which offers an easily graded route into the Vale of Aylesbury. Southwards, too, from Dunstable the valley of the river Ver marks out a route across the Chilterns towards the Vale of St Albans. We may recall here many similar ' gap towns ' of the North and South Downs, such as Dorking, Guildford, Arundel, and Lewes. An additional point of interest in the

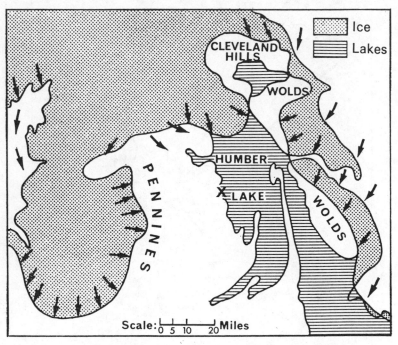

FIG. 39 The Humber Lake during the last Ice Age.
The cross marks the position of Doncaster.

original siting of these towns is their relation to the intersection of old roads which existed before their foundation and helped to define their sites. Thus Dunstable, which became a town only in the Anglo-Saxon period, grew up where the Roman Watling Street crossed the pre-Roman Icknield Way. Roman Verulamium, adjacent to which grew up the later Saxon town of St Albans, was laid out, close to a Celtic tribal centre near by, at the junction of Watling Street with a pre-Roman trackway which led eastwards towards Colchester (Fig. 37).

Similarly, Dorking and Guildford were Anglo-Saxon settlements established at or close to points where Roman roads, built between London and the Sussex coast, crossed the prehistoric Pilgrims Way, which ran east-westwards along the escarpment of the North Downs. The valley site of Dorchester, a Roman foundation which replaced the more ancient hilltop town of Maiden Castle [1] near by, may also have been indicated as the spot where an old ridgeway of the Dorset Downs

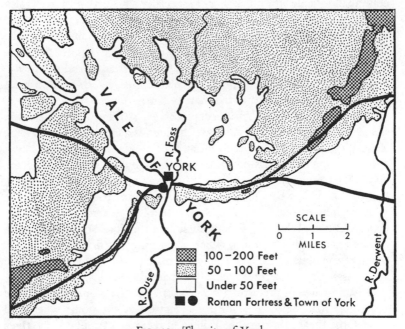

FIG. 40 The site of York.
Of the Roman roads shown, that along the morainic ridge coincided with a prehistoric trackway.

crossed the river Frome (Fig. 38). It is likely that in early medieval times, as certainly in prehistoric times, the east-west ridgeways were more important than the north-south routes, but this is a matter for research.

Another type of site not uncommon in the English lowland may be conveniently described as the ' dry-point site,' since its chief feature was the security which it afforded from floods. Many such sites can be found on rising ground within or marginal to the Somerset Levels,

[1] See above, Chapter V, p. 95.

and within that great tract of fen which formerly stretched through parts of Cambridgeshire, Norfolk, Huntingdon, Lincoln, and eastern Yorkshire. This latter expanse coincided with the area covered by a great lake—the Humber lake, so-called—during the Ice Age (Fig. 39). Two towns which occupy such sites are Doncaster and Ely. The latter stands on an outcrop of Greensand, capped by Boulder Clay : this formed a hill raised above the surrounding flats of peat which were continually liable to inundation, especially if north-easterly gales coincided with periods of high tides and high rainfall. The former arose on rising ground above the banks of the Don at a point sufficiently aloof from the area of low, floodable land which lies to the east. Originally a Roman town on the great north road (Ermine Street), Doncaster, like Cambridge, was so placed that north-south routes could conveniently outflank the marshy flats.

The historic town of York occupies a very striking site. The town stands on a narrow belt of hills which extends across the low Vale of York (Fig. 40). This belt is an instance of a ' moraine,' that is, it was formed from the debris of rocks deposited by ice sheets of the Ice Age. The morainic ridge offered the most convenient route across the vale, and thus between the Yorkshire Wolds to the east and the Pennine hills to the west. To the north of it, where Boulder Clay covered much of the vale, woods, including the Forest of Galtres, were extensive, and to the south, where lacustrine silt floored the plain, passage was obstructed by stretches of marsh. Actually a prehistoric road passed along the morainic ridge from the Wolds, which was an outstanding area of prehistoric occupation, and the Romans, doubtless using this road, selected a site for a fortress at the point where the river Ouse breaks through the ridge and receives a tributary, the river Foss. Like Doncaster, York had the advantage of accessibility by river to small seagoing ships, which could reach the town by way of the Humber and the Ouse. Once founded, York became an important route focus : until the 1790s, it possessed the first bridge across the Ouse,[1] and resort to a ferry was necessary if a traveller wished to cross this river below York.

We cannot explore further the many varieties of urban sites of inland towns. It is remarkable how in England these are commonly

[1] In the 1790s a wooden ' leaf bridge,' which opened to allow the passage of ships, was built across the Ouse at Selby below York. If a motorist today wishes to cross the Ouse below York, he can either pay toll at Selby or cross at either Cawood or Goole.

related to rivers.   Some are natural fording points, such as Wallingford, an Anglo-Saxon foundation on the Thames.[1]   Others, such as Sheffield, stand at a point where streams converge.[2]   Others, again, such as Norwich and Canterbury, occupy firm raised ground at or near the head of navigation for small seagoing vessels or for river craft. Under contrasted conditions of land forms and climate, however, towns often avoid the rivers, which may be unserviceable as waterways

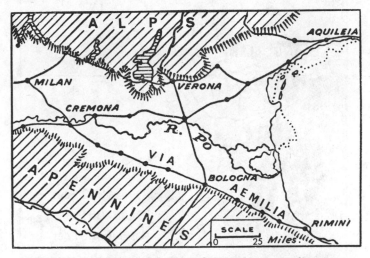

FIG. 41   The distribution of Roman towns in the
North Italian Plain.

*The dotted line marks the present coastline, land having
been built up from the deposits of the Po and other rivers.*

and liable to violent floods.   This is true of many parts of the Mediterranean lands.

We have suggested above that lines of towns can often be traced along the junction of contrasted physical environments.   By way of illustration we may refer to some particular cases shown in Figs. 41 and 42.   Many of the towns of the North Italian Plain are aligned along east-west zones, parallel to the axes of the Alpine and Apennine folding.   Along the arable and well-watered belt at the northern foot of the Apennines the Romans constructed the Æmilian Way and

---

[1] See Hilaire Belloc, *The Historic Thames* (1909).

[2] The convergent streams at Sheffield were significant, not as waterways, but as sources of motive power.

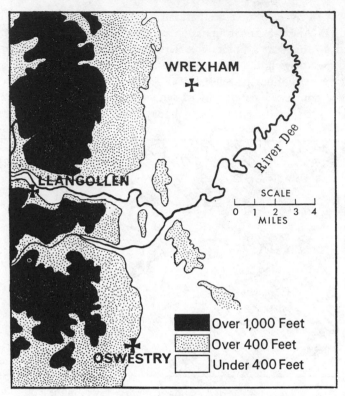

FIG. 42   The position of Llangollen, Wrexham,
and Oswestry.

founded many towns (Fig. 41). These stood on the banks of rivers
which descend from the mountains into the plain, and were well
placed to become markets for the hillmen and plainsmen on either
hand. Significantly there were few towns on the banks of the river Po,
which meanders sluggishly through a broad expanse of marshy flood-
plain. Again, a clearly marked zoning of towns occurs along the
margins of the Central Valley of Scotland where it impinges on the
moorland edge of the Highlands and the Southern Uplands. So, too,
on the Welsh Border, near the junction of the Welsh plateau, with its
sheep runs and its cattle pastures, and the lowland, with its mixed
arable and pastoral farming, we can discover an alignment of towns,
of which Oswestry and Wrexham are representative (Fig. 42). We
may recall also the many foothill and market towns which surround

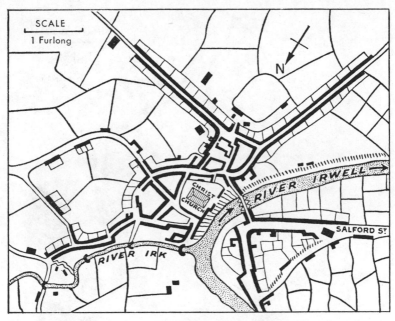

Fig. 43   Manchester and Salford, *c.* A.D. 1650.

*After Aikin's plan.   The nucleus of Manchester, already in Roman times,
lay on rising ground between the Irk and Irwell rivers.   Note the beginnings
of ribbon development and the fields within and around these settlements.*

the high Dartmoor plateau and the two flanks of the Pennine Chain.
Among these are included Leeds, Wakefield, and Manchester (Fig. 43).
The rivers by which these three towns stand, though useless for navi-
gation, are useful in defining well-graded routes up to the plateau.
Finally, if we look farther afield at physical environments unrepre-
sented in Europe, we may note an instance of towns strung out along
the junction of mountain and desert.   Thus in the Tarim Basin of
Central Asia the towns of Kashgar, Yarkand, Khotan, Cherchen, and
Aksu arose on a Piedmont zone of gravels at the foot of mountains in
almost rainless country, which extends into the Taklamakan desert
(Fig. 67, p. 169).   Thanks to springs which issue in the Piedmont belt
and to the streams which descend from the mountains in spring,
irrigation and thus cultivation could be practised in the country
around these towns.

We have argued above that some at least of the functions of towns
seem to be implicit in their sites and positions.   That a town should

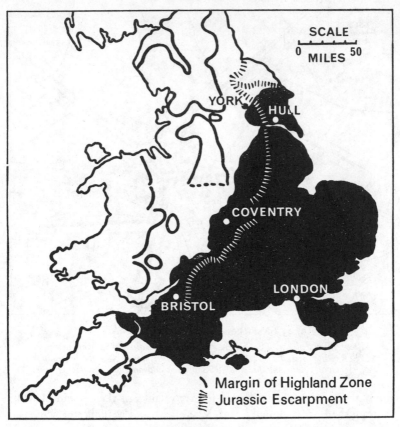

FIG. 44 The most populous area of southern Britain,
c. A.D. 1400.
After R. A. Pelham, modified.

have grown up at or near to Troy seems to have been necessary in
those early times when Ægean seamen were venturing into the Black
Sea by way of the winding, rock-strewn channels of the Dardanelles,
the Sea of Marmora, and the Bosporus. This was a difficult undertaking ; a rapid surface current sweeps through the narrow waters
from the Black Sea into the Ægean, and, except in summer, the prevailing winds are northerly or north-easterly. In the mouth of the
river above which Troy stood ships could find shelter, await favourable
winds, and take in water and supplies. Again, is it true that, owing to
its site and position, London was inevitably marked out as the capital

of England ?   Certainly, thanks to their appreciation of its geographical assets, it became for the Romans the chief route centre of southern Britain when, for the first time, they organised this area as a political unit.   It was York, however, which stood nearer to the Roman frontier, and not London, that provided the capital of Roman Britain, and only in the 12th century did London, or more strictly Westminster, become the more or less permanent centre for the government and the courts. Apart from its advantages as a route focus [1] and as a port, London had also the advantage of standing within a lowland tract which, for reasons of soil, climate, and relief, was potentially and actually the most populous and productive part of Britain in the Middle Ages, when agriculture formed the basis of the economy of this country (Fig. 44). It is remarkable that from the time of Domesday Book (A.D. 1086) until *c.* 1750, when the Industrial Revolution began to alter its distribution, population remained densest in the south-eastern half of England. [2]

'The Fate of Towns and Cities,' said the English antiquarian Camden, ' is every jot as unstable as the state and happiness of Men.' Many instances could be cited to show that physical changes, no less than human vicissitudes, account for the decline or even the obliteration of once flourishing towns :

> Cities that are not and have been
> By silent hill and idle bay.

Bruges, now reduced to mediocrity, though once pre-eminent in north-western Europe, had to yield place to its rival Antwerp, since its waterway approaches gradually silted up and ships sought the safe, deep waters of the Scheldt.   The short-lived town of Ravenser Odd, which enjoyed rather more than a century of economic prosperity, has a sad history which was rigidly controlled by physical circumstances. The site of the town was a small sandbank, which had been built up from marine deposits, close to the headland of Spurn (Fig. 45). Fishermen found it useful for drying their nets and landing their herrings ;   then merchants were attracted there, and such was its prosperity that Grimsby, situated across the Humber, felt its competition sorely and vented its displeasure plainly.   But although it received

[1] See above, Figs. 23, 24, and 25.

[2] See the population maps in *An Historical Geography of England before* 1800 (1936), edited by H. C. Darby.   Recent population movement (e.g. between 1951 and 1961) is adding again to the population density of south-eastern England.

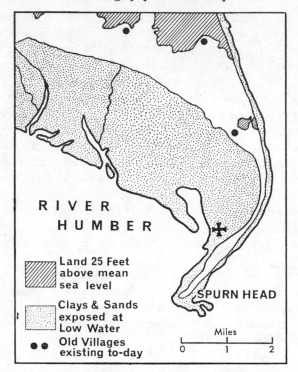

RIVER
HUMBER

Land 25 Feet above mean sea level

Clays & Sands exposed at Low Water

Old Villages existing to-day

SPURN HEAD

Miles
0   1   2

FIG. 45   The former site of Ravenser Odd.
The cross marks the site according to J. R. Boyle, but T. Sheppard argued that it lay to the north-east of the present position of Spurn Head.

a charter from the Crown, and even sent members to Parliament, Ravenser Odd virtually disappeared in the mid-14th century, being drowned by the same tidal waves which had created its site.

Some of the so-called Cinque Ports of Sussex and Kent suffered a fate no less drastic in the Middle Ages.[1] Along these coasts two natural forces were at work which, together with the draining of the marshes, eventually contributed to undermine maritime activity. One of these natural forces was the eastward drift of shingle along the Sussex coast which caused the formation of 'false beaches.' The other was the erosion of jutting headlands by the sea. As a result of this erosion, some towns, notably Old Hastings and Old Winchelsea, originally Saxon foundations, utterly disappeared. Other towns, for

[1] See J. A. Williamson, 'The Geographical History of the Cinque Ports,' *History*, xi (1926), pp. 97–115.

example Rye and Romney, witnessed the gradual shallowing of their deep-water approaches behind the formation of beaches of shingle, and became 'ports of stranded pride.' Seaford suffered the unusual experience of losing its natural haven, as the estuary of the Sussex Ouse shifted westwards, and it lost its maritime functions to Newhaven, which, appropriately named, sprang up during the reign of Queen Elizabeth by the banks of the shifted estuary.[1]

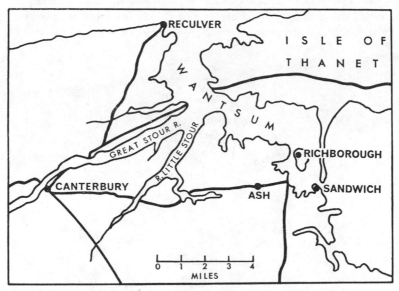

FIG. 46   The Wantsum Channel.
Roman roads are shown.

It would not be easy today to guess that Richborough in Kent was an important naval seaport of Roman Britain, for it lies today well inland and surrounded by low meadows. Its original site, however, was an island within the Wantsum Channel, which was then a tidal waterway dividing the island of Thanet from the mainland (Fig. 46). The drift of shingle formed a bar which blocked the eastern entry to the Wantsum, near which stood the Saxon seaport of Sandwich. As a result of the shingle spit, the Great and Little Stour rivers, which drained into the Wantsum, deposited their silt in the Channel; nor were the tidal waters able to scour it effectively. In the mid-15th

[1] See F. G. Morris, 'Newhaven and Seaford,' *Geography*, xvi (1931), pp. 28–33.

century there was more mud than water in the Wantsum; the sheltered waterway disappeared, and reclamation converted it into useful pastures:

> Where Argosies have wooed the breeze
> Simple sheep are feeding now.

We need not enumerate here many other instances of similar adverse changes. The fate of Chester, which was well placed at the seaward margin of the Midland Gate of England to serve as a port for Ireland, was virtually sealed from the mid-15th century onwards owing

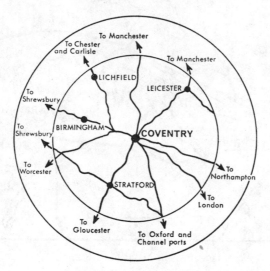

FIG. 47   Coventry as a route focus in the
17th century.

to the accumulation of sands in the estuary of the Dee. Even some of the seaports of non-tidal seas suffered comparable adversity. Ravenna and Aquileia, great Adriatic seaports of imperial Rome, are now inland settlements, cut off by drained marshes from the sea. Changes in rainfall in semi-arid areas, in co-operation with human factors, may account for the decay or abandonment of towns. The busy trading city of Palmyra, for example, which lies on the eastern plateau of Syria, despite its great vigour and wealth in the 1st century A.D., suffered utter eclipse, as a result not only of the commercial competition of Egypt but also, perhaps, of a phase of greater aridity.

In conclusion, we may refer to Fig. 47, which epitomises our discussion of the changing fortunes of towns. The route facilities of a town do not always or inevitably indicate either its relative importance or the extent and vigour of its relationships with the outside world, but in this instance they are revealing enough. A glance at the road system of 17th-century England shows how much more important was Coventry, an 11th-century foundation, than the old Roman town of Leicester, the Anglo-Saxon town of Lichfield, and the nascent town of Birmingham, the fortunes of which had yet to be made.

CHAPTER VII

Frontiers and Boundaries

Frontiers are indeed the razor's edge on which hang suspended the modern issues of war or peace, of life or death to nations.

LORD CURZON, *Frontiers* (1907)

WHATEVER else it may be, a politically organised territory or state is a geographical entity with a definite location and a more or less definite extent. Throughout history states appear to have been somewhat arbitrarily created, enlarged, or even effaced, yet it is widely if not generally true that they are born and grow as a result of the occupation, settlement, and organisation of land. At all stages of its history a state has more or less known limits where it impinges on territories outside its jurisdiction and control. These borderlands form its frontier, and within them a boundary line may or may not be defined. In the frontier zone are usually concentrated a large part of the defensive forces and strongholds of the state, for the purpose of the frontier is to create a strong frame within which the state may exercise its functions and its citizens may live in security.

The distinction in nomenclature between the frontier as a zone and the boundary as a line is essential to any clear discussion of the limits of state territories. The frontier in this sense appears at all periods of history, but the boundary, which has to be surveyed, drawn on maps, and perhaps also demarcated on the ground, is a relatively recent innovation. The first clear instance of boundary delimitation by treaty is in the 9th century, when the empire of Charlemagne was divided among his three grandsons (Fig. 48), but no clear demarcation on the ground was then made. In 1718 a boundary was actually fixed cartographically between France and the Austrian Netherlands, but even towards the end of the 18th century frontiers were the realities in Europe, and few boundaries were accurately known. With the development of the sciences of surveying and cartography, and with the disappearance of complicated and entangled legal rights to land, it became possible to define the boundaries of states in Europe with some exactitude. But today, when the limits of European states are precisely drawn—as are those of the United States—in other parts of the world, less populous and less surveyed, the linear boundary does not always exist.

How far does geography enter into the study of the frontiers of states ? These, it should be noted, are only one of a number of

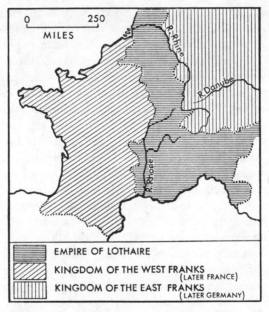

FIG. 48 The division of the Carolingian Empire by the Treaty of Verdun in A.D. 843.

different frontiers with which the geographer is familiar. Some of these are of more direct geographical interest than the political frontier. There is, for example, the physical frontier proper. Illustrative of this type is the tidal delta : like the sea coasts themselves, alternately part of the sea and part of the land, it is a transitional area between two physically contrasted zones. Similarly, the geographer envisages frontiers of climate, of vegetation, and of settlement. In each case, the frontier is usually a transitional area rather than a sharp divide, and since it is an area of land, it becomes a subject of geographical interest.

That the geographical background to state frontiers is a matter of importance, it is easy to see ; the very physical nature of the frontier district is of considerable importance to contiguous states, since this has a bearing on the ease or difficulty of communication, transport, and defence.

If we may assume—and the assumption can scarcely be called cynical—that states always desired frontiers which separated them from their neighbours, we can show that certain types of country best serve this purpose. The best frontiers of separation, especially in the past, were afforded by the oceans, the deserts, mountain systems, marshy tracts, and forests, for the good reasons that such areas set obstacles to human movement and could not support a dense population. The frontiers which the Roman Empire organised against the outside world in the early centuries A.D. were well chosen from this point of view. On its western side the impassable Atlantic washed the shores of Roman Britain, Gaul, and Spain. In the south, the Romans halted in North Africa, Syria, and Palestine, on the margins of the vast deserts of Sahara, Libya, and Arabia. In the east, the Empire bordered the upper Euphrates, where it flows intrenched in the Armenian mountains, and in the north-east it reached, on the northern shores of the Black Sea, the margins of the Russian steppe. It was in continental Europe that the frontiers of the Empire were less defended by nature and ultimately collapsed before the advance of Germanic intruders. The frontiers there lay along or astride two great rivers, the Rhine and the Danube, which, as is usually the case with rivers, were less physical obstacles than means of contact. The Rhine and Danube could be easily crossed ; peoples were settled on both banks, except where alluvial flood plain deterred them ; and further, the rivers were useful for navigation.

So far we have avoided the term ' natural frontiers,' since it is liable to much misconception. It is foolish to suggest that the frontiers of states were predestined by nature, and where real physical obstacles occurred they often failed to become the frontiers of states. Thus, although an island of moderate or small size may seem an obvious framework for a state, it often remained politically divided, as did Britain until 1707. Similarly, the water-parting of the Pyrenees, which divides France and Spain today almost exactly, did not coincide historically with a political boundary. The term ' natural frontier ' is sometimes applied to physical obstacles, such as the Himalayas, which provide great security. It was used also as a cloak to political aspirations, to describe frontiers which would enlarge the state territory.

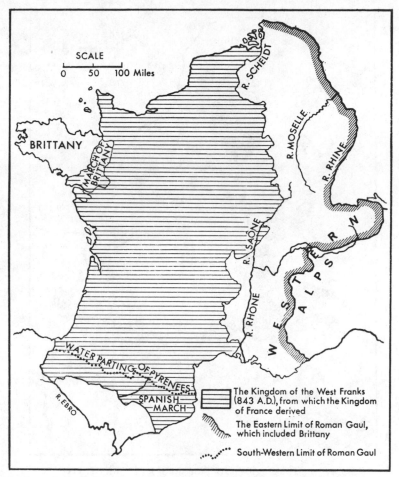

FIG. 49   The limits of Roman Gaul and 9th-century France.

Thus France claimed as its natural frontiers the Rhine, the Alps, and the Pyrenees, which had bounded Roman Gaul, a larger territory out of which France arose in the 9th century (Fig. 49).

We can illustrate from the early Anglo-Saxon kingdoms of England how in early times frontiers tended to coincide with areas of 'negative' land, where communication was difficult and settlement largely lacking (Fig. 50). These kingdoms, some of which, like Kent and Sussex, are represented today by county areas, were bordered and separated by woodland, marshes, moors, and sea-coast. The broad area of marshy

Fig. 50   The Anglo-Saxon kingdoms in the 8th century.
*The shaded area remained Celtic in
speech and in political organisation.*

peat-and-silt flats which lies around the Wash helped to insulate East
Anglia from Mercia ; the dense forests on the wet clay soils of the
Weald, together with Romney Marsh, separated the Jutish kingdom
of Kent from the South Saxon kingdom ; and the most northerly
kingdom of Northumberland, which extended from the Humber
towards the southern shore of the Firth of Forth, had its western
frontier in the sparsely settled tract of high moorland in the Pennines
and the Southern Uplands of Scotland.

In medieval times two frontiers of contrasted physical types divided Britain politically. In the north, the border between England and Scotland corresponded with a broad expanse of bleak upland where population was scanty (Fig. 15, p. 34); in the west, that between England and Wales lay along a lowland zone where intercourse between the two countries took place easily. The Scottish Border was physically a frontier of separation ; the Welsh Border one of contact.

The political unification of Britain was only slowly accomplished, and of the former political units which have become merged in present Britain we are still reminded in many ways—by the administrative boundaries of England, Scotland, and Wales ; by survivals of Celtic speech in Wales and the Scottish Highlands ; and by the increasing national consciousness of Welshmen and Scots. The historical geography of the frontier in Britain presents a great though only partially written theme. We shall attempt here to review briefly from the geographical standpoint the history of the Anglo-Welsh Border.

Let us start with the physical facts. Is there by nature a region, distinguishable from the rest of southern Britain, which corresponds broadly with the present administrative unit of Wales ? The answer would seem to be 'yes,' although the landward limits of this region afford matter for discussion. A broad peninsular area of Britain projects westwards between the estuary of the Dee in the north and the Bristol Channel in the south. But if the form of the coast clearly indicates the limits of Wales on three sides, is its landward boundary physically defined ? Does Wales, as a physical unit, extend to the valley of the lower Wye, or even to the estuary of Severn ? Does it, too, reach up the Dee valley, or even beyond it ? We may note several possible physical limits to Wales on the east. Fig. 30 shows the eastern limit of the outcrop of Palaeozoic or Primary rocks, rocks of great age which occur throughout almost the whole of present Wales but appear only exceptionally as outliers on the margin of the region known to geographers as the English Plain. Is this line significant geographically as well as geologically ? Geologically it is significant since it divided rocks of Primary and Secondary age. Geographically it would be significant only if it divided contrasting physical environments. This, however, is not the case, because for various reasons the eastern, and more especially the south-eastern, part of the Palaeozoic zone provides a habitat different from that elsewhere in this zone. It is characteristically lowland rather than plateau, and enjoys a lower rainfall and better soils.

If next we examine the elevation of the land within the Palaeozoic zone, and if, further, we consider the distribution of rainfall, we can discover a line or lines which are certainly of geographical significance. Fig. 30 shows clearly a contrast between plateau and mountainous country which stands largely above 800 feet, and a borderland which is relatively low-lying although diversified by small detached hill

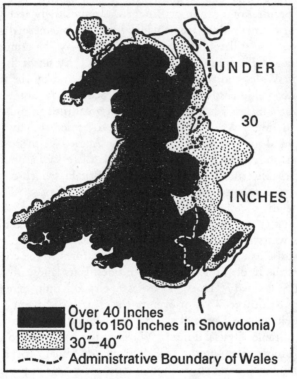

UNDER

30

INCHES

Over 40 Inches
(Up to 150 Inches in Snowdonia)
30"–40"
Administrative Boundary of Wales

FIG. 51   Rainfall map of Wales and the Border.

masses. Fig. 51 emphasises a climatic contrast between the high country which is well watered and the lowland which lies in 'the rain shadow' and receives a much lower rainfall.

Finally, in order to complete our picture of a Wales defined by natural conditions, it is important to assess the bearing of the facts of climate, land forms, and elevation on the economic possibilities of this area. We find here justification for a conception of Wales on grounds of elevation and rainfall. For Wales, as we have defined it physically, is equipped primarily for pastoral farming. Grass grows well on its wet, impervious, and often thin soils, and it is favoured by mild winters. On the other hand, there are many factors adverse to arable farming—the cool summers, the excess of moisture, the poverty of the soils and the small area of plain. If in early days the valleys were wooded and the plateau tops often boggy, there remained wide hilly tracts, plateau sides, and even mountain pastures in summer, which provided grazing for cattle, horses, goats, and sheep. The cultivation of grain, the basis of farming throughout the English Plain, took a very secondary place in Wales. Even in north-west and south-west Wales, especially in Anglesey and Pembroke, where sizeable areas of lowland occur, dairy farming and cattle rearing were important in the Middle Ages as at other times. The traditional grain crop in Wales, as in Scotland, was oats—a hardy cereal well adapted to the local conditions of climate. That there did exist a broad distinction between the means of livelihood in upland Wales and lowland England is exemplified throughout history. Gerald the Welshman, who wrote [1] in the 12th century, gives us a credible picture of the Welsh mode of life :

> Almost all the people live upon the produce of their herds, with oats, milk, cheese, and butter ; eating flesh in larger proportions than bread. They pay no attention to commerce, shipping, or manufactures. . . . The greater part of their land is under pasture ; little is cultivated . . . neither do they inhabit towns, villages, or castles, but live a solitary life in the woods.

So, too, we are told that English soldiers who were campaigning on the Welsh Border in the 13th century grew mutinous because they were given meat and milk, whereas they were accustomed as plainsmen to bread and ale. Finally, as Gerald also related, the typical settlement in Wales was the isolated homestead ; in the English Plain, in contrast, the nucleated village was widely though not exclusively characteristic. That the scattered homestead rather than the village became, as it still is, the more typical rural settlement in Wales is doubtless to be explained in terms of social history, but is not unrelated to the physical conditions—water was available almost everywhere, and pastoral farming, enforced by the nature of the country, was carried on more conveniently from scattered farms. Finally, it is clear that, owing to its poor physical equipment, highland Wales remained at all

---

[1] *The Itinerary through Wales and the Description of Wales*, by Giraldus Cambrensis. (Everyman's Library, 1908.)

times down to the first census of 1801 one of the least populated areas of southern Britain.

In short, we may say that at least on physical ground the lowland belt which extends from Cheshire through Flintshire, Shropshire, Worcestershire, Herefordshire, Gloucestershire, and eastern Monmouthshire constitutes a frontier zone where the Welsh uplands and the English Plain meet and the ways of life begin to change. In these borderlands, owing to the wide extent of clay soils, great forests grew in early times and formed an obstacle to settlers intruding from England. Even so, the lowland border formed a zone of easy intercourse as compared with interior Wales. It was a zone of contact in peace and in war between the peoples from the hills and the plain. Intercourse was facilitated by the fact that it was easier to move from Wales into the border than to move within Wales itself (see Figs. 29 and 30, pp. 70 and 71).

So far we have argued that in physical geography as such there existed two contrasted and contiguous natural regions—upland Wales and the English Plain. When and in what forms did a frontier between distinct states or cultures first appear ? Already in the prehistoric record, as the distribution maps of successive cultures suggest,[1] there are hints of a cultural frontier between the lowland and highland in southern Britain. Peoples and ideas entered Britain on all sides, and of the available entries that into Wales and other parts of western Britain is probably the most ancient (Fig. 27, p. 67). We see indications at different times of loosely framed areas of culture, notably one in the west, co-extensive with Ireland and western Britain, and another based on the English Plain. But there was no hard and fast dividing line, no ' Welsh ' culture confined to Wales alone. In prehistoric times Wales looked mainly seawards towards Ireland, Cornwall, Brittany, and the Mediterranean, but it was not entirely unaffected by cultures established on the English Plain. Yet it is probably true to say that already by the 1st century A.D., when the Romans conquered southern Britain, certain ethnic differences existed between the peoples of Wales and England. Although at that time the whole of the British Isles was occupied by Celtic-speaking peoples, their population was a mixture of many elements which had reached their shores in prehistoric times. Among these, peoples of Mediterranean ethnic type were established in the coastlands of the west, including Wales, and it may be inferred

[1] See the maps in Sir C. Fox, *The Personality of Britain* (1938).

that they entered Britain by its western gateway, for this element was largely lacking in lowland England.

Clear signs of a Welsh frontier appeared during the Roman occupation of Britain. Although the Roman legions conquered England in four years, the subjugation of Wales took them forty years —and this must reflect in part the difficulty of campaigning and the ease of defence in this mountainous and hilly country. Even after its conquest had been effected, Wales remained, as did northern England and southern Scotland, a frontier or military district, distinct and aloof from the Roman civilisation of lowland England. In so far as the Romans left their impress on Wales, they did so by their forts and their military roads, for their towns and ' villae ' [1] were concentrated mainly in southern England and were almost entirely lacking in Wales (Fig. 30). The separateness of Wales from England was emphasised, too, by the woodlands of the Border, within which few Romanised settlements were made.

In the succeeding phase, when England was colonised by Angles, Saxons, and Jutes, the Welsh frontier took more definite shape. The initial stage of the Anglo-Saxon settlement may be ascribed to the period A.D. 450–650, and it is only from this time onwards that it becomes strictly correct to speak of ' England ' and ' Wales.' The word ' Welsh '—' a barbarian appellation,' Gerald the Welshman called it—is derived from the word ' Wealhas ' (or ' foreigners '), which was applied by the Anglo-Saxon settlers to the peoples of Wales, Cornwall, and west Devon. As Fig. 52 shows, Anglo-Saxon colonisation by the year A.D. 650 reached the Severn valley but not the highland zone of Wales. Had these Germanic immigrants spent their force ? Did the mountains and plateaux of Wales appear too uninviting an area for settlement ? Or was the conquest of Wales too hazardous an undertaking ? In any case, when Anglo-Saxon kingdoms emerged later in the lands which had been conquered and colonised, a definite boundary to Wales was demarcated. Offa's Dyke, rightly so-called, was constructed along the western border of his kingdom by Offa, King of Mercia, in the 8th century. It began in the north at a point west of the Dee estuary, and ended in the south along the valley of the lower Wye. These defensive works—a ditch and rampart—were not quite continuous ; they were not constructed in the plain of Hereford where dense forests afforded a natural obstacle.

---

[1] A ' villa ' was a country house or farm.

FIG. 52   The cultural division of southern
Britain, *c.* A.D. 650.

*The area of Anglo-Saxon colonisation is shown black (after
S. W. Wooldridge).   The line of Offa's Dyke is shown.*

Elsewhere, except in Flint and eastern Monmouth, they occupied high
ground, standing at above 800 feet.   West of Offa's Dyke lay Wales,
Celtic in speech and politically divided into several small kingdoms.
East of it stretched the Anglian kingdom of Mercia as far as the
Humber, the upper Thames and East Anglia.   As its name indicated,
Mercia was a 'march' or frontier kingdom, Anglian in speech and
culture, against Wales, the heartland of the western Celtic fringe.
Just how exactly, if at all, Offa's Dyke defined the western limit of
Anglian settlement is not yet clear, although place-name evidence
suggests the abandonment of some English territory in the area north
of the Wye.[1]

[1] F. M. Stenton, *Anglo-Saxon England*, 2nd ed., 1947, p. 212.

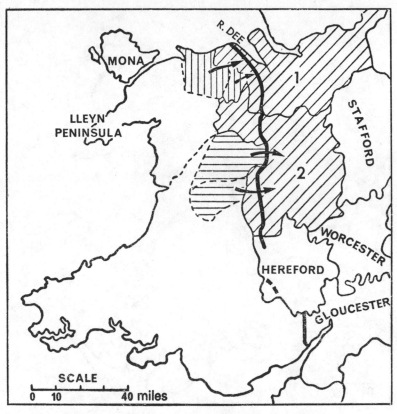

FIG. 53 The marcher lordships of Chester and Salop
in A.D. 1086.
*Marked respectively 1 and 2. The
line of Offa's Dyke is shown.*

To the Normans, as to the Anglo-Saxons, the conquest of Wales
appeared either too difficult or too unattractive a task. Their policy
instead was to create ' marcher ' lordships along the Welsh Border or
within Wales itself ; in return for virtual independence the lords of
the marches were expected to defend the frontier, and, if possible,
extend it at the expense of the Welsh chieftains (Fig. 53). This policy
proved very successful, and as territories were added to the marcher
lordships, castles were built from which to administer them, and
English settlers moved westwards (Fig. 54). Into South Wales particularly settlers immigrated, and English villages, employing the open

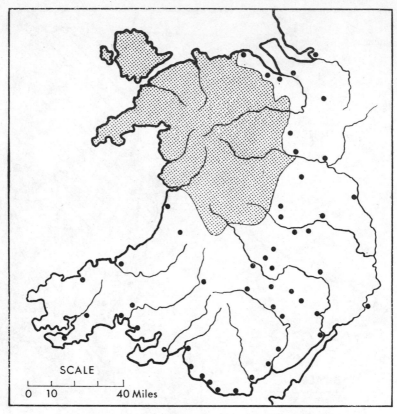

FIG. 54   The distribution of Norman castles in Wales
and the Border.
Gwyned is the area shown black.

field system of Midland England, were established in Pembroke,
Carmarthen, and south Glamorgan.   The distribution of English, as
distinct from Celtic, place-names affords a clue to this colonisation,
and it has been shown that the new English settlements were distributed
mainly in lowland parts of Wales, usually below the 600-foot contour
in the south and the 800-foot contour in Radnor.[1]

The conquest of Wales was completed by King Edward I during
the years 1278–84.   At that time native power in Wales had its base in
Gwyned in the north-west (Fig. 54).   This area, which consisted of

[1] See the maps in W. Rees, *South Wales and the March, 1284–1415* (1924),
pp. 28 and 129.

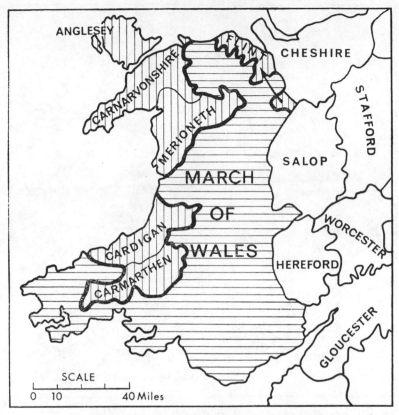

Fig. 55   The new shires formed by King Edward I (shaded vertically)
and the Principality of Wales (enclosed by solid lines).

Anglesey, Carnarvon, and Merioneth, enjoyed two geographical
advantages. It was secluded and somewhat inaccessible, thanks to the
mountains of Snowdonia. Further, it contained in Mona (Anglesey)
and the Lleyn peninsula areas of lowland 'incomparably more fertile
in corn than any other part of Wales.' 'Mona is the mother
(i.e. nourisher) of Wales,' ran the old proverb, and we are told in the
12th century that in the north-west Welsh speech was richer, purer,
and more delicate than elsewhere. Edward created six new shires and
a principality of Wales, which he vested in his eldest son, the first
Prince of Wales (Fig. 55). By 1284, an independent Wales no longer
existed ; the term Wales then connoted the new shires, together with
more extensive areas where the king's writ did not run and the

FIG. 56   The new shires of King Henry VIII.
*The areas shown black were added
to the Border counties in 1536.*

marcher lords held sway.   In so far as a Welsh boundary then existed,
it was defined by the western boundaries of the English counties of
Chester, Salop (Shropshire), Hereford, and Gloucester, some of which
lay farther east than they do today.

The reign of Henry VIII witnessed the final stage in the evolution
of the Welsh Border.   By an Act of Parliament in the year 1536 the
whole of Wales was incorporated politically into the kingdom of
England ; the lands of the marcher lords were divided into shires, and
the limits of the older Welsh shires were modified (Fig. 56).   This
work, in pursuance of the Act, was effected by 1542.   Paradoxically,
the union of Wales with England was signalised by the demarcation of
an Anglo-Welsh boundary, and this boundary, administrative and not

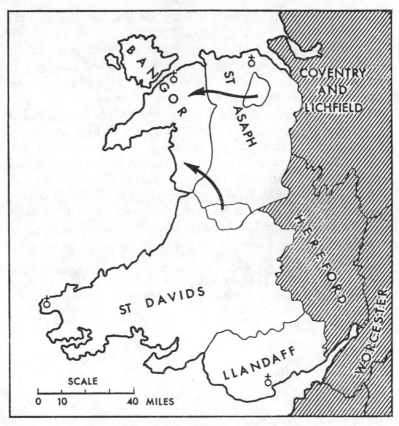

Fɪɢ. 57   The medieval dioceses of Wales and the Border.

strictly political in nature, is that which exists today (Fig. 56).   In
effect, the new Wales was made up of the shires of Edward I, together
with part of the lands long subject to the lords of the marches.
Additions were made to Flint, Shropshire, Hereford, and Gloucester,
and Monmouth was newly created as an English shire.   We cannot
discuss here the bases on which the Welsh boundary was drawn.   An
historian has argued that ' it could not be justified on geographical,
historical, or linguistic grounds.'[1]   Certainly it delimited a Wales
smaller than the area comprised within the marches and the shires of
Edward I., but it is clear that Englishry had made considerable inroads

[1] J. F. Rees, *Tudor Policy in Wales*, Historical Association Pamphlet, No. 101
(1935).

into all sectors of the marches. Still less did it correspond with the larger area embraced within the four Welsh dioceses (Fig. 57). It is not clear how far the new boundary was related, if at all, to the distribution of Welsh and English speech, but we know that by 1536 English had made much headway, especially in the south-west and among the Welsh squirearchy. The translation of the Bible into Welsh, which was printed in 1588, certainly helped to arrest the decline of the Welsh language. However, modern efforts have not proved very successful : whereas half the population of Wales spoke Welsh in 1901 only 29 per cent spoke it fifty years later.[1] But on geographical ground the Welsh boundary is not without significance. Except in Flint and in Monmouth, it broadly corresponds to the line of division between highland and lowland, and that line, we have argued, divided not only contrasted habitats but also different economic and cultural phenomena.

[1] D. T. Williams, 'A Linguistic Map of Wales,' *The Geographical Journal*, vol. lxxxix (1937), pp. 146–51. See also C. B. Fawcett, *Provinces of England*, revised edition by W. G. East and S. W. Wooldridge (Hutchinson University Library, 1961, p. 146).

CHAPTER VIII

Habitat and Economy

' What is it makes a man follow the sea ? '
' Ask me another ! ' says Billy Magee.

C. FOX SMITH, *Follow the Sea*

IT is no longer believed that human communities passed inevitably and chronologically through three economic stages, those of the hunter, the pastoralist, and the agriculturist. Certainly in the Old Stone Age human groups supported themselves by hunting wild animals and by collecting whatever food was afforded by wild plants or could be found by the seashore, and backward peoples survive to this day, as for example, the fast-dwindling Australian aboriginals, who have never outgrown this ' food-collecting ' economy. It would be rash to believe, however, that agriculture invariably came later than stock rearing, and that in particular areas these two forms of ' food producing ' were both adopted, either together or at different times. Rather it is clear that certain lands were suitable for pastoral husbandry, but not for agriculture, although others, more favoured, could be adapted equally to both. In other words, various regions, owing to their physical character, seem to have implied certain modes of life. But between the physical landscape and what may be called the economic response there exists always man, with his particular abilities, desires, and caprice, so that this economic response is not causally related to the physical background. Nature, despite the limitations with which it hedges human initiative and enterprise, is not only very diverse but also remarkably malleable. The geographical link, therefore, between the modes of life of a people and the physical setting, though it clearly exists, is not always so absolute or so self-evident as out-and-out environmentalists believed. Even so, the nature of this link raises interesting problems ; it has been suggested that the intermediary of man's work and the direct consequences of this work constitute the real link between geography and history. And if we can discover the nature of this link we shall be able to understand the place of geography in economic history.

The environmentalist's claim that the mode of life of different peoples is forced upon them by the character of their habitats is clearly an over-simplification of the problem and can be easily exposed. Islanders, for example, do not always take to the sea, however it may appear to beckon them ; neither the Japanese, nor the English, nor the Corsicans cut much of a figure as seamen for many centuries, and in the last case the maritime life has never exercised much attraction. The presence of extensive natural resources of coal and iron, now under active exploitation, has not altered the fact that the Chinese have been, and are, essentially peasants rooted to the soil. Similarly, the great wheat lands of today, in South Russia and the United States, were traditionally grasslands which supported hunting or pastoral economies. On the other hand, no one would safely assert that in the past men chose their ways of life without regard to the potentialities of their country. Accordingly, geographers have come to adopt an intermediate or 'possibilist' position between these two extreme views ; they argue that any given area offers its human occupants certain more or less limited possibilities, from which they choose according to their needs, powers, and whims. Logically this stand-point, which was upheld with much ability by L. Febvre in a stimulating work,[1] is sound enough, but it may well be that the pendulum, swinging away from the old determinism, has swung too far. It is remarkable how in certain parts of the earth, notably in arid or semi-arid areas, nomadic ways of life have persisted with little fundamental change from the dawn of history. Similarly in the cold deserts of the earth a similar uniformity is found in the traditional ways of life. In other words, where climate occurs in forms very restrictive of plant life the range of economic activity permissible to man is similarly restricted. In mid-latitudes, in contrast, where climate is more congenial to plant life, and therefore animal life as well, man has more scope for his efforts and more varied chances of earning his bread or rice.

The fact that very contrasted ways of life were followed in lands not widely separated from each other is well illustrated from the world that was known to the ancient Greeks. With a keen eye to cultural

---

[1] *A Geographical Introduction to History*, English translation (1925).

differences between contemporary peoples, many Greek writers, such
as Herodotus and Strabo, who combined in their works much geographical as well as historical information, concluded shrewdly that
these differences had much to do with environmental differences. The
ways of life of the Greeks, the Egyptians, the Ethiopians, the Persians,
and the Scythians were very different, and no less different were their
geographical foundations. Let us indicate by reference to ancient
Greece and Scythia some particular contrasts in modes of life.

Classical Greece occupied a much smaller area than that of the
present Greek peninsula. Essentially it consisted of a peninsula which
lay to the south of a line drawn between the Gulf of Arta in the west
and that of Salonika in the east, together with many islands (Fig. 1, p. 12).
It was a small, variegated world of sea and mountains, of bare rock and
tiny plains, chequered by nature into numerous small compartments.
Proximity to the interpenetrating sea, its ' Mediterranean ' climate,
and the close association of mountain, hill, and plain—these were the
characteristic features of Greece. Where the land stretched distant
from the sea, where, as in Thessaly or Macedonia, large lowland areas
occurred, and where, too, the climate lost its typical Mediterranean
features, Greek civilisation weakened on the threshold of the ' barbarian ' world. The economy of the Greeks was closely related to,
and drastically limited by, the nature of their terrain. Their greatest
disadvantage was the large mountainous area, consisting mainly of
porous limestones, which occupied about 80 per cent of the surface,
although forests of pine, fir, and evergreen oak, useful for their timber
and rough grazing, covered it more widely in Classical times than
today. Their greatest asset was the climate which, despite summer
drought, permitted the growth of a wide range of useful plants in the
small plains and on the hill slopes. Above all, the Greeks could grow
winter wheat or barley, though not in sufficient quantities for their
needs ; they could grow vines, figs, and olives on the dry, sunny
slopes ; further, by resort to the practice of ' transhumance,' they could
pasture goats and sheep, although the dry, rough pasture was seldom
rich or adequate enough for cattle.

Transhumance, we may note, has always been a practice in Greece,
as in other Mediterranean lands and elsewhere, and though in places it
has had to be given up,[1] it still survives. It registers an interesting case

[1] The use of artificial feeding stuffs and the use of lowland pastures for
cultivation have in some measure militated against the practice of transhumance.

of human adjustment to conditions set by climate and vegetation. On the lower ground, natural herbage was available only in the wetter season of the year, that is, in autumn and winter, for the summers were both hot and dry. On the mountain summits, in contrast, owing to the effect of elevation on rainfall and temperature, pasture was to be had in the spring and summer, although cold and snows precluded its growth during the winter season. Hence a seasonal movement of flocks from lowland to upland pastures became necessary in those days when artificial feeding stuffs could not be provided.

The sea, too, was exploited by the Greeks. It provided them with food, especially the tunny, and with two shellfish which were useful as sources of dyes. The sea provided, also, a relatively easy means of intercommunication, for landwards mountain obstacles everywhere impeded movement, and the rivers, alternatively torrential or dry, were useless for navigation. The Greeks used the seaways too, as traders, for the transport to oversea markets of their manufactured products. In short, the natural environment of Greece was made to yield the material basis for civilised life only as the result of considerable effort, and it has been said that it required the Greeks in Greece to develop Athenian civilisation, and that neither the Greeks elsewhere nor any other race in Greece would have been equal to the task. Classical Greece illustrates also what the German geographer Ritter meant when he argued that certain countries had an educative influence upon peoples.

The country of the Scythians, which was many times greater than the area of Classical Greece, appeared to the Greeks an alien world, remarkable both for its many large and useful rivers and for the great extent of its ' level and deep-soiled plains ' (Figs. 1 and 27).[1] It fronted the Black Sea and the Sea of Azov, from the delta of the Danube to the mouth of the Don ; inland, it stretched a distance comparable with that of its coastline—a journey of some twenty days. In the north, Scythia ended where the south Russian steppe merged into parkland or forest, and where increasing winter cold and cooler summers were experienced. In Scythia, Herodotus noted, more rain fell in summer than in winter : this is a climatic feature untypical of Greece, though characteristic of the ' continental ' régime in Europe.

---

[1] The above account of Scythian life is based mainly on Herodotus' *History*, Bohn's edition (1854). Herodotus wrote in the mid-5th century B.C., and actually visited the coast of Scythia.

The winters in Scythia, too, were long and severe—too cold, in fact, for the baggage animals of Greece, the mule and the ass, but not too cold for the horse, for which the broad, open plains provided a congenial habitat. Much the greater part of Scythia, then as now, was destitute of wood. One curious effect of this, if we can believe Herodotus' story, was that the Scythians used the bones of the ox as fuel in the cooking of its flesh. In their economy they contrasted sharply with the Greeks. They remained staunch to the nomadism which they had brought with them from Central Asia. They drove cattle and horses over the rich pastures of the steppe, and sustained themselves mainly by the milk of mares and by making cheese and butter. In the most southerly parts of Scythia which bordered the sea the people sowed and lived on wheat, millet, lentils, onions, and garlic. Others too, near by, grew wheat, ' not for food, but for sale.' The reasons for this defection from nomadism was doubtless the penetration of Greek cultural influences and the chance and ease of trade in corn by means of the seaways. The great rivers of south Russia yielded, near their estuaries, both sturgeon and salt. The horse was the Scythian means of locomotion, and trade caravans were made up of horse-drawn wagons. For the Scythians, as for nomads generally, overland trade formed an important branch of their economy. It is significant, too, of the nomad's way of thinking and of a strategical advantage that the nomad's way of life enjoys, that the Scythian king informed his enemy, Darius, King of Persia, that he (the former) had no need to force a pitched battle, since, he said, ' We have no cities, nor cultivated lands.' Without fixed settlements—for the movable tent is their usual abode—with their wealth mainly in the form of horses and cattle that can be driven off at need, and with their control of the horse as a means of swift movement, nomads, such as the Scythians, enjoyed a great advantage in defence over sedentary, agricultural folk, much of whose wealth could not be transported to safety, and, if destroyed, could not be easily replaced. The destruction of olive groves in Greece, for example, meant a capital loss, for the trees do not bear much fruit until they have been tended for some twenty years.

It is clear that Scythia, contrasting as it did both geographically and economically with the city-states of Classical Greece, afforded the latter an accessible and fruitful field for trade. Greek cities, which were founded near the mouths of the Danube and the south Russian rivers, served as means of contact and centres of exchange. The

Greeks brought their wine, oil, and manufactures ; the Scythians their corn and hides.

That the typical Greek was a farmer, tending his olive groves, his vineyards, and his flocks, and that the typical Scythian was a nomad or ' a cattle-driver,' certainly reflects the very different settings in which their lots were cast. So much so that Greek writers, and others after them, believed that the physical environment differentiated modes of life. Thus Strabo, noting the great contrast between the material culture of the Egyptians and the Ethiopians, wrote : [1]

> The Ethiopians lead for the most part a nomadic and resourceless life on account of the barrenness of the country and of its remoteness from us, whereas with the Egyptians the contrary is the case in all these respects ; for from the outset they have led a civic and cultivated life . . . both tilling and following trades.

That Egypt owed very much to the Nile floods the Greeks had always been well aware, and Strabo knew that these were not so much ' heaven sent,' as Homer put it, as the result of summer rains in Ethiopia.

But we cannot deduce from the physical environment alone— however fully we study its climate, relief, soils, mineral deposits, position, and so forth—what forms its economic life took at particular periods. From a physical survey alone we can make only tentative statements about the past economy. We can say that in a given area certain things could be produced, others could not be produced, and yet others could be got only with difficulty or by importation. We can say that physical conditions made transport easy or difficult in certain directions, either by water or by land. We can know for what means of livelihood the area seems naturally best fitted. We can assert that climate usually ordains at what season permissible crops must be sown. But when all is said it is very evident that the human factor, which varies from people to people and from time to time, gives its particular stamp to the economic life. Nature imposes ; man disposes. But man's action is doubly limited—by his own abilities and by physical possibilities. The physical environment, which appears to set finite limits to the activities of human groups at any particular time, has in fact potentialities which expand or contract in relation to the material culture of these groups. Every terrain, in fact, is a different

---

[1] Strabo, *Geography* (Loeb edition, by H. L. Jones), vol. viii, p. 9.

terrain to every folk which may inhabit it. It is scarcely axiomatic that every terrain gets the folk which it deserves. We need only recall how the cultural ability of present-day peoples ranges from that of Stone Age culture to that familiarly known as Western Civilisation to realise that any given area would be exploited very differently by different occupants. Not only would men follow in varying degrees different modes of life, but the actual surface of the area would present different cultural features.

Let us inquire more closely what are the geographical limits to economic activities. The distribution of minerals, including petroleum, is fixed by nature ; where such resources are lacking, all that men can do is to devise substitutes or effect exchanges with other areas suitably endowed. Actually the exchange of metals seems to have begun as early as Neolithic times, and the succeeding culture of the Bronze Age implied the transport of either copper or tin, since these essential constituents of bronze seldom occur together in the same areas of the Old World. Again, the sources of power which provide the basis of modern industrialism are either rigidly localised by geology, as in the case of coal and petroleum, or depend for their production on physical conditions, as in the case of hydroelectric power. Even the energy of the tides and gales, which, on a long view, may become the motive power in the future when coal and oil supplies have been exhausted, has an uneven distribution from place to place.

In respect of the products of vegetation, which furnish both food supplies and raw materials, physical factors, and above all climate, impose themselves as important conditions. Indirectly, as well as directly, men are dependent on vegetation, for this provides the food-stuffs for animals, which are useful in many ways—as food, as beasts of burden, as motive power, and as sources of raw material. The distribution of natural vegetation, so called, a map of which is useful in the study of an area, bears little relation to the vegetation cover which obtains today, except perhaps in some parts of the tundra, desert, and equatorial zones,[1] where human interference has been most difficult and least effective. Thus the former forest cover over the greater part of the United States has been largely removed, especially during the last hundred years (Fig. 58). But the map of natural vegetation is valuable historically in that it outlines realistically the

---

[1] It is believed that very little of the tropical forest of Africa today is, strictly speaking, primitive.

scene of man's early activities : it throws light on his ease or difficulty of movement and on his chances of exploiting the soil. The distribution of natural vegetation bears a close relationship to the disposition of climatic belts. Similar climatic conditions, however, do not everywhere reflect similar natural vegetation, for plants have not been able to move with equal freedom from place to place. The same is true of animal forms ; although there are distinctive genera associated with particular tracts of vegetation, different types of wild animals are found

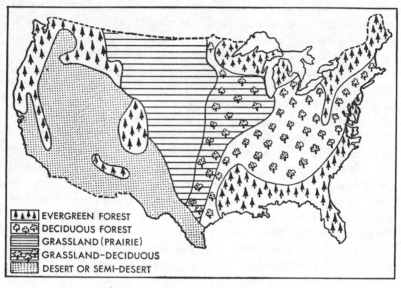

FIG. 58 The vegetation cover of the United States *c.* 1800
Much generalised.

in areas of comparable vegetation. The New World, too, shows a remarkable poverty of natural fauna.

At least from Neolithic times, man began to modify the fauna and flora of his habitat. On the one hand he waged war on certain forms of vegetation and animal life, and on the other he began to cultivate certain wild plants and to domesticate certain animals. His opportunity to do these things differed much in different climatic zones. In the far north of Eurasia, for example, climate allowed man little chance either to cultivate or domesticate. In these high latitudes, where the subsoil is always frozen, the growth of trees and grain was impossible, and the scanty natural vegetation—lichen, a few shrubs, and a little grass in summer—could support only a few animals, notably the reindeer, which man learnt to domesticate and use for many purposes —for milk, meat, draught, burden, and riding. No less were his chances restricted in low latitudes where the wild luxuriance of tropical forest, resultant from the combination of great heat and abundant moisture, imposed a masterful obstacle in his way, the more so since it supported and concealed a vigorous fauna and insect life fraught with danger. It was in parts of those extensive lands which lay between the hot and cold deserts that human enterprise had most scope, particularly in sub-tropical lands where a dry season imposed a check on the growth of vegetation and insects. These lands offered to man a large balance of advantage in respect of vegetation. Owing to the seasonal pause in the growing season, forests did not widely attain that impenetrability characteristic of equatorial latitudes, and further, these mid-latitudinal lands were well stocked with varieties of wild trees and other plants, together with animals, some forms of which were potentially useful to man and, as events proved, were capable of domestication. Finally the climate permitted in some of these lands two or even three crops a year. Thus in southern Japan, under monsoonal conditions of climate, which consist of a hot and rainy season following a mild and rather dry winter, two cycles of life were possible in the year.

We can distinguish several broad areas where plants, cultivated by man, grew in a wild state before the dawn of civilisation, although it is not yet clear which was the original homeland of some of our more important plants, such as bread-wheat and barley.[1] Soft wheats, rye, certain varieties of flax, vegetables, and fruit trees, including the vine, were native to Asia Minor, Persia, Transcaucasia, and certain parts of Central Asia. In the Mediterranean lands, including the coastlands of Asia Minor, Palestine, and Syria, there were few wild plants useful for cultivation—the oleaster or wild olive, the fig, emmer wheat, a coarse variety of flax, and a few vegetables. Some experts believe that Abyssinia was an early home of hard wheats, barley, and coffee, and that this was the source of the barley and wheat which were cultivated in Egypt at an early date:[2] certainly it is remarkable how many varieties of wild grain occur today in Abyssinia. Tropical India, again, can claim as native plants rice, sugar cane, and certain varieties of cotton. To the mountainous parts of eastern and central China the

[1] See also on such problems Chapter X above, pp. 153 and 158–60.
[2] See below, Chapter IX, p. 141.

orange, lemon, peach, mulberry, tea, soya bean, millet, and oats originally belonged. Finally, native to the intertropical parts of the New World were a number of plants which are now cultivated widely, notably maize, cotton, tobacco, tomatoes, and potatoes. The last actually grew, too, in equatorial parts of South America, since on the lofty Andean plateau climate is so modified by elevation as to make possible the growth of this temperate plant.

It should be noted that each group of plants did not occupy necessarily those areas where climate was most favourable ; nor did they occur in all the areas where their growth was climatically possible. It is significant of the uneven distribution of plants within areas climatically suitable to their growth that whereas flax, but not cotton, grew in Egypt and Mesopotamia in Neolithic times, cotton, but not flax, grew then in the Indus plain of north-west India. Similarly, although different areas, on account of their topography and vegetation, were especially suited to particular domesticated animals, these did not appear in all such suitable areas. This was due partly to the competition between different genera of animals, and partly to the lack of facilities for widespread migration. Thus the horse appeared early on the open steppes of Central Asia and on the more confined grasslands of Europe, but his later appearance in Arabia and north Africa was due to man.

It is remarkable how very few types of animals and plants have been respectively domesticated and cultivated. It may be true to say that men learnt to cultivate all the plant forms which repaid their efforts, and that they domesticated, though often for originally non-economic reasons,[1] as many animals as were economically profitable and practically possible. Once the arts of domestication and cultivation were mastered—these processes were mostly effected some five thousand years ago in the Old World—people were able to exploit economic potentialities of their habitats which had hitherto lain dormant. They introduced new plants and animals, acclimatising them doubtless by the method of trial and error. Thus most of the characteristic plants of the Mediterranean lands today were introduced at different periods. Bread-wheat, the cultivated olive, the vine, the citrus fruits, the mulberry tree, and many hard fruits were established there through the agency of Greeks, Romans, Arabs, and later peoples. Similarly, in lands of modern colonisation new food and industrial

---

[1] It is believed that the initial domestication of animals was usually for ceremonial or ritual purposes. The domesticated turkey of Mexico, for example, was a pet with ceremonial uses and was seldom eaten. See C. D. Forde, *op. cit.*

crops have been introduced over wide areas, and have displaced the former cover of vegetation.

The acclimatisation of plants in lands of which the conditions of climate and soil were little known invariably led to many failures, and even today a pioneer farmer in the United States must venture warily unless he has learnt what climatic irregularities and other local conditions obtain. But the difficulties involved in exploiting new lands often evoked inventive effort. A graphic story is told[1] how, in the first half of the 19th century, Scottish settlers attempted to cultivate the prairies around Winnipeg. Almost unbelievable obstacles beset their enterprise. Myriads of migrant birds, clouds of grasshoppers, and Indian bands preyed upon their crops, which, moreover, were not at first suitably adapted to the local climate. But their efforts were eventually rewarded, since they discovered varieties of wheat suited to the short growing period. More recently, varieties of wheat have been produced which can be grown in the Canadian prairies in as little as a hundred or even ninety frost-free days. In this way Canadians have outwitted climate in some measure and have been able to extend the frontier of cultivation northwards into lands formerly dominated by forest. Similarly, in many parts of the world—in California, Spain, Italy, Soviet Turkestan, and India—resort to irrigation has converted stretches of arid waste into highly productive land. But natural conditions have to be considered in effecting schemes of irrigation. First, the products of irrigated land must, as a rule, be able to compete successfully with those of unirrigated lands elsewhere ; second, the indispensable water must be obtainable during the growing season ; third, the quality of the soil and the slope and subsoil of the terrain must be suitable to irrigation.

In so far as plants and animals have particular biological requirements, the economic production of any area was restricted by nature. The climatic limits to the growth of plants are sometimes rigid, as in the case of the olive, and sometimes flexible, as in that of the mulberry tree. In any case it can be shown that a plant has both optimum and permissive limits to its growth. That is, it can be grown more successfully in certain areas within the greater area where its growth is possible. The truth of this is very evident today when, given the existence of a world market for many products, a great deal of specialisation in geographically favoured areas occurs, notably in North

---

[1] Sir J. Russell, *The Farm and the Nation* (1933), pp. 97–102.

America. This truth applies too, though in smaller degree, to the past.

The cultivation of the vine in western Europe and the silk industry, dependent on the mulberry tree, may serve to illustrate how certain industries were localised in the past. The vine was certainly cultivated, if only sporadically, well to the north of the present limit to its growth (Fig. 59). Introduced into southern France by Greek colonists and

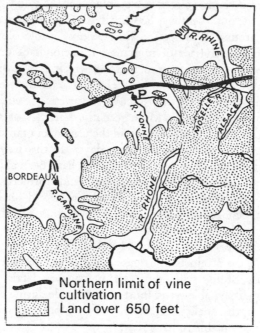

FIG. 59 The present limit of viticulture
in France.

later extended by the Romans as far north as Alsace and the Moselle valley, the vine was grown around Bruges in the later Middle Ages and, as Domesday Book records, in many parts of southern England. Even so, a tendency to specialisation in viticulture in certain favoured areas had already set in during the later Middle Ages. Thus the villagers in the district of Auxerre on the upper Yonne river in France 'neither sowed nor reaped,' but concentrated on growing vines and making wine. That they were able to do this is explained by geographical factors : the river afforded convenient and suitable transport for wine, which was liable to deteriorate if carried along ill-surfaced roads, and further, the river led down-stream to the Paris market. Similar on a larger scale was the vineyard area behind Bordeaux. The river Garonne and the port of Bordeaux served in the shipment of wine, much of which was sent to England, the kings of which ruled Gascony for two centuries of the Middle Ages. Wheat had to be shipped to Bordeaux, since, through specialising in the vine, the local people did not produce sufficient grain for their own needs. In short, although the vine was widely grown in western Europe, where conditions of climate, soil, and slope allowed, the availability of water transport to good markets produced something like monoculture in certain places.

The story of the silk industry is similarly instructive. The rearing of the silk moth was once the monopoly of central and southern China, where alone the highly skilled craft of silk-making was understood, and where the mulberry tree, under the conditions of monsoon climate, had two cycles of life a year and thus produced two supplies of fresh leaves. Now the mulberry tree is very tolerant of climate ; it will grow as far north as Norway and as far south as the Equator. It is tolerant, too, of soils, except that it will not grow in areas that are too clayey or marshy. Once the delicate processes involved in sericulture were learnt,[1] the making of silk could be attempted widely in Europe. Actually, the rearing of the silkworm has been restricted to parts of southern Europe—Greece, Italy, southern France, and Spain. Close study shows that climate was in fact a restrictive factor. It is necessary that the weather is free of frosts when first the moth appears in spring, and further, that a supply of fresh mulberry leaves is then ready. These conditions obtained broadly in the Mediterranean lands, except at high altitudes, but not farther north in continental Europe. Even if by artificial means the right temperature for the hatching of the moth is provided, the mulberry leaves appear too late in the north. When we recall, too, that in the Mediterranean lands only one crop of leaves a year can be got owing to the summer drought, it will be seen that they did not enjoy such natural advantages for this industry as did China and Japan, and to this day these countries, and above all Japan, retain the chief place in the production of raw silk.

[1] See below, Chapter X pp. 174 and 176.

CHAPTER IX

The Dawn of Civilisation

Ease is inimical to civilisation. . . . The greater the ease of the environment, the weaker the stimulus towards civilisation.

A. J. TOYNBEE, *A Study of History*, vol. ii (1934)

The districts where civilisation began probably had at that time the most stimulating climate in the northern hemisphere.

C. E. P. BROOKS, *The Evolution of Climate* (1922)

IT would be rash to believe that the beginnings of civilised ways of life have been fully revealed to us, but, thanks to archaeological discoveries of quite recent times, we know a great deal about them—infinitely more than was known to the Graeco–Roman world. It is clear that the land or lands which appear to have cradled civilisation have been unequally explored by the archaeologist. Even Egypt has not been thoroughly explored, and other lands, potentially of great importance, await fuller scientific excavation. In northern India spade work has only just begun, and is yielding remarkable results ; and in Mesopotamia numerous prehistoric sites have not yet been laid bare. Asia Minor, northern Syria, Persia (Iran), Central Asia, and China are to a fair extent unworked fields from which rich crops may yet be reaped. But if in a generation's time our view of the beginnings of civilisation may need considerable revision, it is nevertheless true that reasonable hypotheses may already be made.

Let us be clear by what signs we distinguish ' civilisation ' from the many cultures of a more primitive kind. Archaeologists argue convincingly that Neolithic culture represents the first culture which may fitly be called ' civilised.' During the many millennia when peoples lived at a Palaeolithic or epi-Palaeolithic stage, they remained largely at the mercy of a physical environment which they had little power to control. They won their livelihood by hunting, fishing, and food-collecting, and were ignorant of food-producing by means of agriculture and the domestication of animals. By the exercise of great creative effort Neolithic folk, during the period from 6000 to 3000 B.C., invented new ways of life. The economic basis of Neolithic civilisation was food-production by cultivation and by pastoral farming. Its social expression was first the village, to which was added later the town. In craftsmanship many original advances were made : Neolithic folk learnt how to make wheel-turned pottery and kiln-fired bricks ; how to spin wool, cotton, and flax, and to weave fabrics therefrom ; how to work metals and to build on a monumental scale ; how to write and to devise a calendar ; how to trade and to organise states, and how to fashion works of art. The appearance of some or all of these evidences of civilised life at the Neolithic stage shows that people then possessed a new, if incomplete, power to adapt the natural environment.

Where did Neolithic civilisation first appear ? The answer is : Egypt and Lower Mesopotamia, to which in every probability north-west India must soon be added. Civilisation appears then to have been born either near, or on the banks of, four great rivers—the Nile, the Euphrates, the Tigris, and the Indus. Which of the riverine civilisations can claim precedence in time is not yet clear, for the earliest finds in Lower Mesopotamia and Egypt may be roughly contemporary. In fact, some experts hold that civilisation probably arose spontaneously in these three regions. Was there a region of yet earlier civilisation from which these received cultural stimuli, as a result of the movements of peoples, or of the flow of ideas and practices ? Those who believe that such was the case look towards northern Syria and eastern Asia Minor as likely centres. On the other hand, there is no valid reason for believing that human inventiveness could not appear independently and spontaneously in several similar areas. The answer to our problem turns on the part which ' diffusion ' has played in prehistory. Must we assume that there was only one source of civilisation whence the light was diffused elsewhere ? There are many objections to this extreme diffusionist view—notably the fact that many civilised practices, for example writing and agriculture, developed in Central America long before it was brought into relation with the Old World.[1]

We need not pause to examine further the diffusionist problem.

[1] See below, Chapter X, pp. 158–61.

What is more important to our purpose is that the first traces of civilisation appeared in a few regions of distinctive physical endowment at an unascertainable date, about and probably earlier than 5000 B.C. It is our task to define clearly the geographical settings of this momentous human revolution, and then to inquire how far their nature may explain why civilisation arose there when it did.

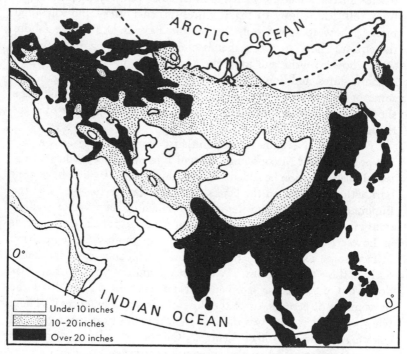

FIG. 60   A generalised rainfall map of the Old World.
The Afrasian steppe-desert belt coincides with the area
which receives less than 10 inches of rain annually.

Before we examine particularly the riverine lands of Egypt, Lower Mesopotamia, and north-west India, we must note broadly the great tract of country within which the lower courses of these rivers lie. It is conveniently described as the Afrasian steppe-desert belt, itself part of a more extensive arid belt which extends across the Old World from the Atlantic to northern China (Figs. 20 and 60). The Afrasian steppe-desert belt consists structurally of a number of rigid, tilted crust-blocks, alike in north Africa, in the Arabian peninsula, and in

Iran (Persia). These present generally plateau levels, except where a few major depressions and young fold mountains occur. The chief depressions are the alluvial flats through which pass the lower courses of the Nile, the Euphrates, the Tigris, and the Indus rivers. The chief mountains are those which border the Iranian plateau on the west and the east, the Lebanons in Syria, and the Atlas ranges in north Africa. Climatically the whole belt, including the riverine lands, is character-ised today by an almost complete lack of rain, by hot summers, and by mild winters. The riverine lands themselves were physically analogous ; each consisted of an alluvial plain, bordered by desert or mountains or both, and open on one side to the sea. In each case, too, and this was clearly a factor of first-rate importance, the great river or rivers carried into the region from wetter areas in their upper basins copious supplies of water at one season of the year.

We have already discussed the question of past climates in the Afrasian steppe[1] (Fig. 20, p. 46). We argued that, for many millennia prior to the final disappearance of the Scandinavian glaciers about the year 6000 B.C., the Afrasian steppe–desert belt, especially on its northern side, enjoyed a moderate rainfall all through the year, and presented as a result a vegetation cover of grass together with some trees. After *c.* 6000 B.C., the climatic belts shifted north to their present position, and the grasslands suffered gradual desiccation under climatic conditions similar to those of today. Hence the period when civilisation arose and developed in the riverine lands falls almost entirely within the period of present climate, and it is significant that the earliest finds there may coincide roughly with the transition from raininess to drought. Just how close this coincidence was we cannot be too sure, since we are dealing with dates of a very loose kind, the one based on geological, the other on archaeological evidence. As we shall see, the earliest Neolithic sites in Egypt suggest that the rainy period was not quite over. But, as we argued above,[2] there is every reason to believe that the first effective colonisation of the riverine lands was made at a time when the Afrasian grasslands were becoming too dry to sustain life for all the hunting peoples who dwelt there. There is a further climatic consideration to which we shall refer later on, namely that, despite the onset of dry conditions, there seems to have been a slightly higher rainfall during the last few millennia B.C. than obtains today.

[1] See above, Chapter IV, pp. 46–7.
[2] See above, Chapter IV, pp. 48–9.

For the moment we shall examine the past geography of the riverine lands.

But for its numerous historic and prehistoric sites and all that these have revealed, Lower Mesopotamia in its present condition has little to suggest the outstanding part which it has played in world history. This area corresponds roughly with the present kingdom of Iraq, which is notable today for its resources of petroleum, not for its agriculture.

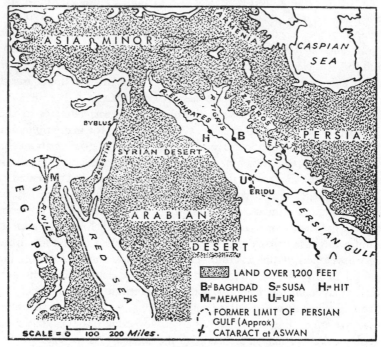

FIG. 61   Egypt and Mesopotamia.

Lower Mesopotamia forms the southern part of what archaeologists have called 'the Fertile Crescent,' namely, the lowland which extends from Palestine to the Persian Gulf on the flank of the deserts of Arabia (Fig. 61). Today great areas of Lower Mesopotamia, as a result in part of centuries of neglect by its Turkish rulers, are either treeless, waterless, and barren wastes or undrained marshes. But an accumulation of evidence both literary and archaeological testifies to its former productivity and to the amazingly precocious civilisation which it sustained during a period of several millennia before Christ.

Lower Mesopotamia is a broad, alluvial plain, of about the area of Great Britain, which lies between and eastwards of the lower courses of the Euphrates and Tigris rivers. Northwards it extends as far as Beled on the Tigris and Hit on the Euphrates, where beds of limestone outcrop in the river bed and obstruct navigation. Structurally, Lower Mesopotamia is a ' sunk-land ' : it was formed parallel to the faulted edge of the Arabian crust-block, when the Zagros mountains were folded in Tertiary times. The trough then created was subsequently filled up by masses of detritus carried down and deposited by the Tigris and Euphrates, and by spring torrents which descended from the Zagros mountains of western Persia ; even wind-borne sands from the Arabian desert added also their quota. Further, alluvium was deposited at the outlets of the Tigris and Euphrates, with the result that a considerable area of marshy land was built up at the expense of the Persian Gulf. Since the dawn of civilisation the head of this Gulf has receded seawards perhaps as much as 150 miles (Fig. 61). Some of the earliest prehistoric sites, notably Ur and Eridu, which now stand far inland, originally stood on the margin of the Persian Gulf. Thus the land was built up from transported rock waste of neighbouring lands ; similarly, the early peoples of Mesopotamia included elements which intruded chiefly from the desert, but also from the mountains and the sea.

The Euphrates and Tigris collect a great volume of water from their upper basin in the Armenian mountains, where melted snow in spring supplements the run-off of rain. The Tigris receives, too, additional waters from the mountains of western Persia. Lower Mesopotamia is almost rainless ; Baghdad, for example, has nineteen rainy days a year, and a variable rainfall, mainly in winter, which averages about nine inches annually. The spring floods were therefore indispensable to cultivation in Lower Mesopotamia. These could be very violent and even catastrophic, and it is more than probable that Noah's flood, described in Genesis, actually occurred in Sumer, the lowest part of Mesopotamia. The Tigris–Euphrates floods occur at a different time from those of the Nile and necessitate a different form of irrigation. In Egypt the floods begin to rise in June, rise rapidly in July and August, and remain high during September, and ' basin irrigation,' so called, was necessary. The floods were allowed to spread over the alluvial plain and drain back to the Nile ; then seeds could be sown —even without tillage—and the soil remained sufficiently moist during the growing period. In Lower Mesopotamia, on the other hand, the floods occurred in March, April, and May, and were followed by a rainless, scorching summer. Crops could not be grown after the floods unless resort was had to irrigation ; hence something similar, of a rudimentary kind, to the perennial irrigation which is practised today in Egypt and Sind, had to be undertaken. Such an expedient involved the need of storing and distributing water, and it thus called for well-organised efforts and technical skill. But if these works were undertaken, even in small areas of the plain, two crops a year could be grown and good yields won, for the winters were mild and almost frostless and the best of the alluvial soils were light calcareous loams, rich in plant foods. Moreover, the silt-laden waters of the Euphrates and the Tigris, especially those of the latter, helped to renew the fertility of the soil, although, when in flood, they deposited coarser materials than the fine-grained silt of the lower Nile.

As waterways the Euphrates and Tigris had only limited value. If the rocky bars across these rivers, respectively at Hit and Beled, obstructed navigation, they served at least to impound water, and these natural reservoirs were improved and utilised in very early times. Both rivers could be navigated below these points, but they were difficult for up-stream traffic, since their currents, especially that of the Tigris, were strong, and their banks were unfit for towage. The date palm was indigenous to Mesopotamia, and emmer—a variety of wild wheat which, together with barley, has been found there growing wild —was certainly cultivated as early as the fifth millennium B.C. Stone, timber, and bitumen, which were lacking in the alluvial plain, were obtained from areas near by. From Elam, the foothill area to the east of Sumer where the earliest sites have been found, timber and stone were carried into the plain, and bitumen was brought down the Euphrates from Hit. Other products, too, such as wine and oil, as well as minerals, especially copper, and spices, were brought there by traders. Some of the early settlements, such as Ur and Eridu, stood on the desert margin of Sumer and may well have functioned as desert ' ports.' The beast of burden which served the earliest inhabitants was the ass ; the one-humped camel and the horse were not introduced into Mesopotamia until relatively late in the prehistoric period.

Throughout its long recorded history Egypt consisted of the alluvial lands of the valley and delta of the Nile below the first cataract of Aswân. Although this area was continually divided into two or more kingdoms or provinces, it consisted of two permanent natural units. Upper Egypt is the long, narrow valley section, which varies in breadth from a maximum of twelve miles to a minimum, above Thebes, of less than two miles   Lower Egypt is the triangle of delta, which was built at the expense of the sea by river-borne silt, and is fringed by lagoons and sand dunes on its seaward side   Upper Egypt, the flood plain of the lower Nile, is not strictly speaking a rift valley, as is the Jordan valley ; nevertheless it lies deeply sunken between high cliffs of limestone or sandstone on either side (Fig. 62).   The lower Nile was navigable as far as Aswân, where masses of granite occur in the river bed.   Boats could move down-stream on the river's usually gentle current, and up-stream navigation was helped by the northerly

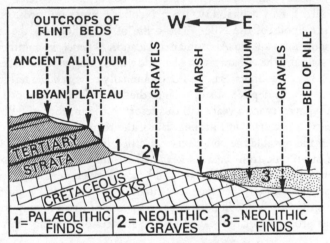

FIG. 62   Half-section of the lower Nile valley
above the delta.

winds (the Etesian winds of the Greeks) which are prevalent mainly in summer.   Deserts, in which many scattered oases occurred, bordered the alluvial plain on both sides, and the high desert ridge was broken by numerous ' wadis,' which are today waterless.   On its eastern side, high desert, known as the Arabian Desert, itself a fractured part of the great Arabian crust-block, stretches to the Red Sea, to which it presents a rocky and arid coast, scorched by the summer sun. On its western side, at a lower elevation, but no less arid, extends the Libyan Desert, through which, however, two routes are defined by nature ; one lies behind the low, sandy, inhospitable coast, where there is a slight rainfall ; the other, far inland, is marked by a zone of oases which permit travel by stages. The deserts insulated Egypt, but were in no sense an invulnerable shield—the nomadic peoples who dwelt there were tempted continually to intrude into the settled agricultural plain of Egypt. The eastern desert, too, offered routes to the Red Sea ports and towards Palestine and Syria. The Mediterranean itself afforded means of communication with Crete and Syria, at least as early as the mid-fourth millennium B.C. Finally, in the south, where the Nile waterway ceased, a tract of desert separated Egypt from Nubia, an area of grassland and woodland, which remained a cultural backwater.

Practically rainless, except for a small fall in the Nile delta, Egypt depended for its habitability, from Neolithic times onwards, on the summer floods of the Nile. The cause of these floods is the heavy monsoon rains of the Abyssinian highlands, whence in summer the Blue Nile and the Atbara rivers bring down copious waters. In Egypt, as in Lower Mesopotamia, the floods annually renewed the fertility of the soil by the deposit of silt, so that the land could be cropped continually, even twice a year, without resort to the practice of fallowing which was necessary in Europe. But if the regular inundations of the Nile made possible the continuity of settled life in Egypt, their variations in volume from year to year had serious results. An excessive rise inundated villages and towns and caused much devastation, and a deficiency of flood water spelt lean times or even famine. At all times the distribution of the flood waters was a task of first-rate importance, and its proper regulation called for the services of a strong centralised state.

The rich black soils of Egypt promised high yields. The proverbial corn of Egypt, as early as pre-dynastic times,[1] was barley, millet, and emmer wheat—for bread wheat was introduced only in Roman times. The flax plant was grown very early; the papyrus reed, and probably the date palm, were indigenous. From papyrus not only Egyptian paper but also the earliest boats were made. The alluvial plain lacked timber, since after the drying up of the Afrasian steppe-desert belt, useful timber trees disappeared; so, too, it lacked metals, especially copper and iron. Many of the crops which appear in the course of Egyptian history, such as cotton and sugar cane, were introduced there relatively late, but the olive grew on the western margin of the delta as early as about 3000 B.C.

---

[1] That is, before *c.* 3400 B.C.

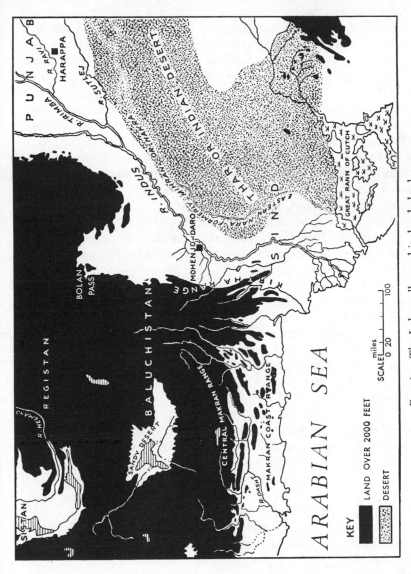

FIG. 63   The Indus valley and its borderlands.

The last level bridge between the continents lasted between 33,000 and 9000–8000 B.C.

Finally, the archaeological discoveries of this century have revealed a third primary centre of civilisation, namely the riverine plain of the Indus in Punjab and Sind, where the physical conditions were strikingly similar to those of Egypt and Lower Mesopotamia. The alluvial plain of the Indus was flooded and fertilised in early summer by the waters of the Indus, and, it is believed, by those of a great sister river, which were fed by the melted snows of the Himalayas. Already in the third millennium B.C., as archaeological evidence convincingly shows, people lived in constant dread of the Indus, which has always been notorious for its violent floods and its continual changes of course in the low, alluvial plain. The floods were perhaps not so severe when the first towns arose in the valley, for the sister river to the Indus, the Mihran, carried the greater volume of water along a course parallel to, and eastwards of, the Indus [1] (Fig. 63). To the east of the alluvial lands, the desert of Thar, and to the west, mountain ranges and high steppe-lands, emphasised the geographical individuality of the riverine plain.

In order to complete our sketch of the geographical background to the early civilisations nurtured in the riverine lands, it is necessary to try and picture them, not as they appear today, but in the natural state in which the first settlers found them. Herodotus' familiar dictum 'Egypt is the gift of the Nile,' although it has obvious truth, can be very misleading, for the Egypt of history was no less the gift of man. Today, as already in the Roman period, Egypt presents an essentially 'humanised' landscape, in that it has been drastically modified by long periods of human effort. Similarly, the fertility of the Fertile Crescent was the result of strenuous 'colonial' activity. The riverine lands, as they appeared to the first intruders from the neighbouring deserts or highlands, were subject to both the devastations of flood and the limitations of drought. There were wide areas, especially in the deltas, of dreary and perhaps pestilential marsh ; wide areas covered by thick, high reeds ; and there were vestiges at least of the jungle vegetation, together with its animal denizens, which had flourished during the rainy period prior to *c.* 6000 B.C.

There is a great deal of evidence to suggest that during the last five millennia before Christ the rainfall of the riverine lands, though less than that of the preceding pluvial period, was rather greater than it is today. The fact that Egypt and its bordering deserts were able to support a fauna and flora which must now be sought in lower latitudes,

---

[1] See above, Chapter IV, p. 54.

e.g. in upper Nubia, suggests that the rainfall was higher and the herbage more plentiful than they are today. The first settlers of Egypt found there not only hippopotami, crocodiles, wild boars, and great numbers of wild fowl of various kinds, but also, in the neighbouring oases, elephants and gazelles. In Dynastic times, that is, after *c.* 3400 B.C., there existed a wide variety of wild animals which included the lion, the antelope (its chief prey), the gazelle, the ostrich, the wild ass, and the Barbary sheep. The subsequent disappearance of these animals from Egypt and the north African deserts suggests the continued drying up of the oases, although human agency played some part.[1] Similarly, early Egypt boasted more tree species than it does today— the sycamore-fig, two varieties of palm, the acacia, the sunt, and the tamarisk ; moreover, in the earliest stages of settlement, as finds of tree roots and charcoal at Faiyum and Badari indicate, some useful timber trees and brushwood grew on the now arid margins of the alluvial lands. Further, experts have shown that the water level of Lake Mœris in the Faiyum depression, though falling, stood much higher during the millennia 6000–3000 B.C. than it does today. When we consider also striking evidence from Baluchistan and the Indus valley, it is clear that the higher rainfall was not a purely local condition. Numerous large and flourishing villages from which agriculture was practised, as well as immense dams, have been found in southern Baluchistan, in country which is now so dry that it can support only nomadic peoples. It has been plausibly argued that the higher rainfall in Baluchistan and the Indus plain, which was not very plentiful or too well distributed throughout the year, was due to the fact that the monsoons were then effective over a wider area. Such an explanation is eminently reasonable, since other similar marginal shifts of the monsoons seem to have occurred. On the other hand, the contemporary raininess in the African steppe-desert belt must be attributed to Atlantic rainstorms which would have reached Baluchistan and to a lesser extent north-west India.

As a result of this light raininess, which was insufficient to mask the fact that climate had become much drier than hitherto and to make irrigation unnecessary, the riverine lands possessed a rich flora and fauna at the dawn of civilisation. This was in part an aid, in part an

---

[1] Thus it is suggested that the introduction of camels into North Africa by the Arabs drove the lion southwards by restricting the pasture available for the antelope and other animals on which the lion preyed.

obstacle, to the pioneer settlers, for they had to combat wild animals, to clear the land of reeds and jungle, and to drain the marshes. We may sum up the environmental conditions of that time by suggesting that nature gave and withheld her gifts with equal restraint. If Egypt, the Indus valley, and Lower Mesopotamia—where some would place the Garden of Eden—were regions of superfluity in respect of food supplies, this was not a natural gift but the result of well-directed and concerted efforts to adapt and exploit the natural endowment. Let us glance very rapidly at the archaeological record to see by what stages, and with what skill and creativeness, the riverine lands were mastered and utilised. Let us have in mind, too, how very important in human history were the events then enacted in those lands.[1]

The earliest Neolithic finds have been made in Egypt and in Elam, which borders Lower Mesopotamia, although there is reason to believe that discoveries of similar date may be made in the Indus valley. Already, *c.* 5000 B.C., the inhabitants of the village of Susa in Elam made wheel-turned pottery and linen ; they had copper axes and polished flint implements ; and they were probably acquainted with agriculture, although they depended mainly on hunting. Many mounds or 'tells,' which have been built up from the accumulated remains of successive villages of mud-and-reed huts and stand out today above the level of the plain, mark the sites of successive Neolithic villages such as Susa. Thus already in the 5th millennium B.C. the first cultural revolution had taken place in Lower Mesopotamia, and also, as we shall see, in Egypt. It was characterised by the appearance of village life, agriculture, the smelting and working of copper, and the manufacture of textiles and pottery. If we move forward rapidly and survey the scene about 3000 B.C., great advances in technical skill, and in social and economic organisation then appear, and the second revolution has occurred. Instead of small self-sufficient villages of folk engaged chiefly in hunting, we find cities of considerable area, the inhabitants of which were engaged not only in agriculture but also in specialised crafts and in external trade. Monumental buildings, chiefly temples, were built of kiln-fired bricks ; irrigation was practised by the building of dams and the cutting of canals ; and silver, lead, gold, and lapis lazuli came into common use. The Sumerians, too, had invented a solar calendar, and pictographic writing on clay tablets. Moreover, they possessed a number of domesticated animals—cattle,

[1] See above, pp. 74–5.

sheep, and asses—although the actual domestication of these may have been achieved by neighbouring hillmen or steppe-dwellers rather than by the plainsmen themselves. It is clear that Sumerian civilisation presupposes external trade, or if not that, at least the carriage of products from other, often distant, lands—copper from Oman, shells from the Persian Gulf, lapis lazuli from Afghanistan ; silver and lead perhaps from the Taurus mountains of south-east Asia Minor ; and timber from the Zagros mountains. Similarly, certain products of Sumerian craftsmanship are known to have reached cities in the Indus valley. Finally, we may note that the cultural achievements of the peoples of Lower Mesopotamia were made under a city-state organisation. A territorial state, coextensive with the Fertile Crescent, was created by Sargon *c.* 2500 B.C., a task more effectively accomplished by Hammurabi some five hundred years later.

In Egypt the earliest known Neolithic settlements, which may be dated some centuries earlier than 5000 B.C., stood on the northern rim of Lake Mœris, which lies in the Faiyum depression south-westwards of Cairo. Great interest attaches to the discoveries made at Faiyum :

> In the Faiyum Neolithic granaries, of which we found 117, we appear to have the earliest evidence for corn-growing yet known, though from what quarter they originally obtained their knowledge and the seed-grain of wheat and barley remains obscure.[1]

Some centuries later there are signs of a similar civilisation in the Badari area, which extends from the desert spurs across the alluvial plain to the Nile. The Badari folk, in whom a negroid strain has been detected, were more or less settled—they grew barley and emmer wheat ; kept cattle, goats, and sheep ; wove linen ; used copper, unavailable locally, and Red Sea shells. It is significant that their settlements stood near the wadis which flowed into the alluvial plain.[2] Much later, about 3500 B.C., the valley and delta lands of Egypt were united into a single kingdom, and the capital was fixed at Memphis, just above the head of the delta where passage across the Nile was facilitated (Fig. 61). Already, under King Menes (*c.* 3400 B.C.), a Nilometer was used to measure the height of the Nile floods, of which

---

[1] Miss G. Caton-Thompson and Miss E. W. Gardner, ' Recent Work on the Problems of Lake Mœris,' *The Geographical Journal*, vol. lxxiii (1929), pp. 40–1.

[2] It is not yet clear whether they cultivated the alluvial plains, for the alluvium may cover up evidences of occupation.

records were kept. It is clear that in Egypt, as in Lower Mesopotamia, a flourishing agriculture supported a dense population, permitted the accumulation of capital, specialisation in many crafts and professions, as well as an active foreign trade. Limestone and granite were quarried locally and transported along the Nile ; either copper or turquoise—it is not clear which—was brought from mines in the Sinai peninsula ; cypress, pine, and juniper wood, together with resin from the Lebanon mountains, reached Egypt by sea from Byblos in Syria ; and gold and spices were brought from Nubia.

In the Indus valley, the prehistory of which is rather less well known, an urban civilisation, comparable with that of Lower Mesopotamia and Egypt, has been revealed both at Mohenjo-Daro and Harappa (Fig. 63). The finds in these towns are dated about 2500 B.C., but it is known that earlier settlements existed there. Mohenjo-Daro was a large town, with an area of one square mile, that is, twice the area of Roman London ; its streets conformed to a plan ; two-storey houses, including workshops and shops, were built of kiln-fired bricks and provided with sewers ; many specialised crafts existed, and statuary of great artistic excellence was fashioned. Whether or not they were indigenous to the region, wheat, barley, dates, and a coarse variety of cotton were produced there, and the domesticated animals included pigs, sheep, cattle, humped bulls, and water buffaloes. The riverine lands of Sind and Punjab certainly formed a culture province, but it is not known whether they were ever organised as a single state. Goods reached these lands from areas outside ; deodara cedarwood from the Himalayas, dried fish from the sea coast, and many minerals and precious stones from places much farther afield. Moreover, certain manufactured articles from the Indus towns, especially square seals, found their way into the villages of Baluchistan, and even to the cities of Sumeria.

We cannot discuss the problem how far the civilisations of Lower Mesopotamia, Egypt, and the Indus valley were independent local growths. It is believed that these urban civilisations were not transplanted from one centre to another, but were rather organic growths rooted in their respective soils. That is not to say that they did not show many similar cultural traits and did not hold intercourse with each other, notwithstanding the great distances which separated them, whether by land or by sea.

In conclusion, let us return to our second question : how far does the physical nature of the riverine lands explain why civilisation arose there when it did ? Let us make clear at once that we do not attempt to explain the genesis of civilisation as the inevitable outcome of the conditions of physical environment. A. J. Toynbee called attention to other riverine lands, allegedly analogous, in which no contemporary civilisation emerged, and although the instances which he adduced were not so analogous geographically as he implied, he had no difficulty in disposing of this explanation. Further, he argued that it was the sheer difficulty of the environment in the riverine lands which challenged its first settlers and evoked there a remarkable response. Stimulated—not daunted—by drought, flood, swamp, and wild animals, the first settlers, by their own creativeness and enterprise, conquered their difficult environment and introduced there the arts of civilised life. In short, according to A. J. Toynbee, ' the greater the ease of the environment, the weaker the stimulus towards civilisation.'

This view is no less extreme than that of the environmentalists, and is in many ways unsatisfying ; nor does it explain why in some areas the physical challenge was met and in others ignored. It is clear that every terrain is a different terrain to every folk which it supports, but the extent to which, and the way in which, peoples adapt and exploit their physical environment is conditioned and limited by physical facts. If, as seems probable, men first settled the alluvial lands as immigrants from the drying grasslands of Afrasia, they were offered there natural advantages as well as drawbacks. Drought, flood, and marsh, it is true, were obstacles in their path. On the other hand, the rich alluvial soils, the indispensable river floods, the long growing period, the river route-way, and the indigenous plants and fauna—all these could be turned to good use. It may be open to discussion whether, as C. E. P. Brooks suggested, the riverine lands enjoyed the most stimulating climate of the northern hemisphere at the dawn of civilisation, although we have shown that they were not so arid as they are today. Further, it may well be significant that the riverine lands were surrounded in each case by physically contrasting regions—desert, mountains, or sea—whence came peoples familiar with other ways of life and other products and ideas. In so far as the contact and intercourse of peoples thus differentiated were stimuli to creative thought and action, the folk of the riverine lands were in this respect geographically well favoured. It may well be that their civilisation represents not only the product of their own creativeness but also the pooling of the inventions and experience of neighbouring peoples.

CHAPTER X

The Dawn of Civilisation in the Americas

. . . it is not always true that necessity is the mother of invention. If it were true, then inventions ought to have been made in places where the struggle for existence was very hard. But instead they are made where conditions of life are easy.

ERLAND NORDENSKIÖLD, *The American Indian as an Inventor*

WE are well aware of the major divisions of the Americas and of the increasingly important parts which they play in world affairs. These are : North America, not to be lightly subsumed as ' Anglo-America,' for this includes Cuba as well as the United States and Canada ; Middle America, which includes Mexico together with the isthmian territories and the islands of the Caribbean Sea which constitute Central America ; and South America, which, a continent in its own right, forms the bulk of what is familiarly known as ' Latin America ' by reason of its cultural associations with Spain and Portugal. Although in respect of their nationalities and cultures the Americas appear in large degree as extensions of Europe, and in their economic cast as the products of recent centuries, they have nevertheless their own distinctive histories, overlain and obscured though these appear to be by the events and processes which followed the settlement of intruders from Europe. The problems which focus on the origins of man in the Americas and on the dawn of civilisation there clearly engage the interest of the archaeologist, historian, and, among others, the geographer too.

The American Indians, despite earlier contacts made by Viking seamen [1] in the 11th and 12th centuries, became widely known only

---

[1] Viking sagas refer to ' Skraelings ' armed with bows and arrows and using boats made of skins. These are thought to have been Eskimoes. Archaeological

five hundred years later by Columbus and his successors : their origin baffled Europeans then, as it poses problems not yet solved. When first discovered by the Spaniards and Portuguese, the Amerinds were clearly of mixed and varied ethnic types. In facial colour alone they range from yellowish brown to chocolate brown : ' Redskins ' and ' Red Indians ' are loose if picturesque simplifications. ' Could they conceivably be descendants of Adam and Eve ? ' was the first question to be asked. Its answer in the affirmative led to many different explanations, *inter alia* that they were descendants of Phoenicians, of the ten lost tribes of Israel, of Tatar-Mongols. Such explanations, which involved speculation about the lost continent of Atlantis, found literary expression down to the 19th century. For us, mindful that no such continent has existed since the Tertiary era, when the Atlantic Ocean took its origin, i.e. long before the advent of man, the questions, for scientific treatment, persist : when and where did the Amerinds originate ? And had they precursors of distinguishable ethnic type ?

The Old World has been perhaps too ready to acclaim the youth of the New ; the New World has not lacked claimants for a less junior rôle in the history of mankind. In particular, discussion has turned on the question whether man was present in the Americas before or only after the Great Ice Age had ended. This discussion cannot as yet reach an agreed conclusion since it depends on the findings of several sciences which have still far to go. In particular, an answer depends on what is known, and what is further to be revealed, about the Great Ice Age, or Pleistocene period, which is regarded by some geologists as the closing phase of the Tertiary era and by others as the first phase of the Quaternary era.

The Pleistocene period witnessed successive advances of ice sheets from the north over large areas of Europe, Asia, and North America and also the advent of man, one surviving subspecies of which (*Homo sapiens*) ultimately emerged—and survives. There were several successive phases when the ice sheets advanced. They were followed by periods when the ice sheets retreated and climate became less severe ; the last phase—known as the Wisconsin stage in North America and the Würm stage in Europe—was followed by the post-

confirmation of the presence of Vikings now seems forthcoming : it was reported in March 1963 that the remains of a house of Viking construction had been excavated at Lance aux Meadows in northern Newfoundland. In 1964 the U.S. Government gave official recognition to the Vikings as first discoverers of North America.

Fig. 64 The Bering Strait and the Alaskan threshold of North America.
The last land bridge between the continents lasted between 33,000 and 9,000/8,000 B.C.

glacial period—which may be also an inter-glacial period—in which
we now live. No firm basis exists for measuring the total length of
the Pleistocene which may be reckoned of the order of 800,000 years.
And it is by no means easy, especially in North America, to assign
dates to its end. Further, we are warned that, despite the broad
comparability of onset and withdrawal of the ice sheets which exists
between the New and Old Worlds, 'post-glacial time differs from
region to region.'[1]

It is agreed that until nearly the end of the Wisconsin stage of the
Pleistocene, North America was joined to north-east Siberia by a broad
and low plateau area now occupied by the Bering Strait and parts of
the neighbouring Bering and Chukchi Seas (Fig. 64). This junction

[1] J. K. Charlesworth, *The Quaternary Era* (1957), vol. ii, p. 867.

was the result of the lowering of the sea level by a few hundred feet consequent on the locking up of so much water in the thick continental ice sheets. Further, the lower parts of Alaska, mainly in the interior but also in some of its coastlands, were never wholly covered by ice. Similarly it is believed that parts of northern Siberia, through lack of precipitation, were free of ice sheets. During inter-glacial periods, when climate was less severe, certain grasses and animals in turn migrated into North America by way of Alaska and spread south-wards.[1] As noted above for the Old World (p. 46), so also in the Americas, the broad pattern of regional climates then must have differed from that of post-glacial times. The lowered sea-level, too, had evident effects on the drainage of low-lying lands. Obstacles, such as the Mexican and Peruvian deserts and the tropical lowland swamps of the isthmus of Panama, did not exist in the forbidding form which they assumed in post-glacial times. A wide range of animals was thus able to move into South America through the Central American isthmus, which modern travellers have found a formidable task. They included mastodons, mammoths, giant sloths, armadillos, glyptodons, as well as camels, horses, musk-oxen, mountain sheep, goats—and wolves. This diverse fauna came to differ specifically and generically from those of the Old World. Moreover, though late-comers to the Americas, the giant animals showed the ability to survive longer there. It is known on reliable evidence, for example, that an extinct form of bison still lived in New Mexico and also a mammoth in Mexico as recently as 4,000–4,500 years ago.[2]

Only near the close of the Wisconsin stage, in the millennium 9000–8000 B.C., was North America sundered from Asia by the creation of the Bering Strait : this seems to have been due to the rise in sea-level which followed the melting and withdrawal of the ice sheets. The Bering Strait contains a number of islands, and narrows to a width of only fifty-six miles ; during exceptional winters, a broad waste of frozen seas still joins the two continents together.

It is clear that *Homo sapiens* alone has inhabited the Americas, which

[1] The movement of animals across the Bering Strait area and the Panama isthmus was in both directions. Thus, for example, the horse, native to America (where he died out), migrated to Asia, only to return to America with the Spaniards.

[2] P. Rivet, *Les Origines de l'Homme Américain* (Paris, Gallimard, 4th ed., 1957), pp. 34–5. The period 8000–3000 B.C. witnessed the extinction of most of the large Pleistocene mammals in the Americas, for reasons that are obscure.

were not the home of his precursors, nor indeed of the anthropoid ape. It is no less certain that the first inhabitants of the Americas co-existed for many millennia with fauna which in Europe appeared in the Tertiary era yet were Pleistocene intruders into the New World. It is known, too, beyond doubt that Palaeo-Indians, so-called, as distinct from the Amerinds of later time, occupied successively North, Central, and South America as far south as Patagonia at the end of the Great Ice Age. Discussion persists, however, on the date of man's first coming to North America. Did he first appear, as Rivet [1] firmly argues, at the end of the Pleistocene, about 10,000 years ago, or, as Lothrop [2] believes, as early as even 35,000–50,000 years ago. The former view has long been orthodox as it is also conservative ; the latter opens new perspectives as it remains yet to be proved. The solution of the problem will clearly turn on the evidence which steadily grows : very much more doubtless has yet to be discovered which should eventually permit firm conclusions.

Contributions to the solution of this problem come from a variety of independent scientific sources. Palaeontological studies—concerned with fossil man—as well as geological, archaeological, and anthropological studies share a common interest in trying to establish the time sequence of their discoveries in relation to the layers in which they are found. Happily a new and wholly independent means of dating the past has been made available by the radioactive carbon (C^{14}) method. This technique is applicable to certain organic materials, such as wood, charcoal, and peat, and can succeed in revealing their age, reliably up to 15,000 years, less so up to 30,000 years. [3]

As yet there is no bulk of evidence to support the view that man entered North America in Pleistocene times. No human skeletons exist which are older than 12,000–15,000 years. Three specific sites have, however, yielded evidence indicative of man's presence 20,000–30,000 years ago. At Tule Springs, Nevada, charcoal believed to be of human origin is dated as more than 23,800 years old. [4] The burnt bones of a butchered mammoth at Santa Rosa Island (California) are

---

[1] P. Rivet, *op. cit.*

[2] S. K. Lothrop, ' Early Migrations to Central and South America : an Anthropological Problem in the Light of other Sciences,' *Jour. Roy. Anthr. Inst.*, vol. xci, part 1 (1961), p. 119.

[3] F. E. Zeuner, *Dating the Past* (2nd ed. revised, 1950), pp. 337-8, 401-2. See also Geoffrey Bushnell, ' New World Chronology,' *Antiquity*, vol. xxxv (1961), pp. 286-91.

[4] W. F. Libby, *op. cit.*, p. 121.

reckoned about 30,000 years old, while at Louisville, Texas, stone artefacts are thought to be more than 37,000 years old.[1] While Carbon[14] dating is unreliable for objects of such great age, further evidence is to be expected. As Sauer [2] put it, ' Pleistocene man can no longer be denied ; it is only a question as to how far back his title extends in America.' The other view [3] is that American man cannot date very far back into Pleistocene and appears only in its closing phase.

The Palaeo-Indians of the Americas, distinguishable by their artefacts, were widely established some 10,000 years ago. It may well be that we should visualise several periods of immigration from north-east Asia across the broad land connection established during the last (Mankato) phase of the Wisconsin stage, and the last may well have brought most of the intruders. Climate then was severe, if less so than earlier, and intruders doubtless needed to be clothed. Palaeo-Indian artefacts found in western and central Alaska suggest that this was the threshold of the New World, although it has not yet yielded reliable C[14] dates of great age. With the withdrawal of the glaciers, zones of passage southwards, with grazing facilities, appear to have opened up through British Columbia on the seaward and eastern flanks of the Rocky Mountain system. Some anthropologists believe that the Palaeo-Indians were a long-headed people ethnically distinct from the Amerinds of later time, yet, for reasons that are obscure, very few of their skeletal remains have been found. Their artefacts of stone include primitive types comparable with those of Lower Palaeolithic culture in Europe as well as others more expertly made. These are the pressure-chipped, vertically fluted, and smoothed stone points which are peculiar to the Americas. They have been found widely and mostly in North America, then the culturally most advanced part of the New World. This culture—in European terms—can be called Upper Palaeolithic or, as Sauer would claim, Mesolithic. Yet it remains a matter for speculation how these men battled against the animals, many of which were outsize, which they hunted and on which they fed. They are not definitely known to have possessed propulsive weapons, such as the spear-thrower and the bow, although they doubtless used their ability, in suitable terrain, to launch fire drives.

[1] S. K. Lothrop, *op. cit.*, pp. 102–3.

[2] C. O. Sauer, ' A Geographic Sketch of Early Man in America,' *Geog. Rev.*, vol. xxxiv (1944), p. 539.

[3] M. Boule and H. V. Vallois, *Fossil Men* (London, 1957), p. 485.

Immigration into North America, by way of Alaska, has been the orthodox view since Hrdlicka's studies earlier this century. This view first rested on the similarities between Mongoloid ethnic types found both in the Americas and in Asia. It may expect to find increasing support as archaeological knowledge of northern Asia increases. It finds some support in the proven relationship between certain Amerind languages and some of those of northern Asia.[1] Thus the widely spoken Quechua language, the official language of the Incan empire, is related to the Turkic language family. And a widely spoken Indian language of North America—Na Dene—is similarly related to Chinese or Sino-Tibetan. Modern studies of blood groups, however, suggest no simple and close affinity between American Indians and Asian Mongoloids ; rather they suggest the survival in the Americas of old and pre-Mongoloid racial stocks. Similarly the variety and complexity of Amerind cultures seem to argue in favour of an earlier beginning of immigration than was once thought likely and also of migration from many parts of Asia, even though this was funnelled through Alaska.

What stage of culture had been reached by these intruders from Asia, who, little though they realised it, first discovered America ? This has been described as that of 'the higher savagery' of Upper Palaeolithic times, which, at its highest terminal phase in the post-glacial period, is now distinguished as 'Mesolithic culture.'[2] Ignorant of agriculture, without domesticated animals and without any knowledge of pottery-making, textile crafts, metals, and building, they were by no means lacking in the ability to survive and populate a wide variety of climatically contrasting environments. They knew how to live in forests, to make fire and to collect food, and to organise hunting. They came to learn how to make and use boats and to fish, fashioning a range of implements and weapons of wood, bone, ivory, and stone. The impulse behind the migration into America may be seen in the withdrawal of ice-sheets from northern Europe and Asia which presented a new world for colonisation by forests and by men. It is Mesolithic man, with his skills as a forest-dweller and a fisher-hunter, who pioneered in this new and seemingly hard environment, eventually taking North America into his stride. And the scale and range of his movements in the Old World were repeated in the New, being related doubtless to the mobility implied by hunting economy.

[1] P. Rivet, *op. cit.*, pp. 78–82.
Grahame Clark, *From Savagery to Civilization* (1946), chap. iii.

While the main prehistoric immigrants into the Americas seem clearly to have come from Asia by way of Alaska, we are no longer so sure as formerly that the New World was wholly isolated from human contacts made across the flanking oceans. Thor Heyerdahl [1] has assembled abundant evidence to support the view that in pre-Columbian days the Peruvian balsa-log raft, rigged with cotton sails, was capable of sailing to Polynesia, carried there by the easterly trade winds and the south equatorial current : his Kon-Tiki expedition in 1947 indeed was his most convincing evidence. Such a movement might explain the alleged transfer to these islands of several cultivated plants, including the sweet potato, the bottle gourd, and the coconut palm. Paul Rivet [2] has presented a case for human movements in the reverse direction which may have brought intruders to America from Melanesia, thousands of miles away, at a remote date in the past, perhaps some 4000 years ago. The evidence advanced to support this admittedly difficult geographical operation is various. It relates to anthropometric and blood-group data, cultural affinities and identities, certain virus diseases, and, more impressively, the alleged relationship between the Hoka language family with Malayo-Polynesian. Amerinds within a large area of the Americas between latitude 3° N. and 43° N. spoke this language, 281 roots of which appear identical with Malayo-Polynesian forms.

The possibility and feasibility of a small-scale drift of people across the tropical Atlantic have also been urged as an explanation of the existence of a Caucasian-like element in the pre-Columbian population of the Americas—men with white skins, heavy beards, and reddish-brown hair.[3] Actually West Africa and South America at their closest lie only 1,700 miles apart ; the Canary Islands, when first discovered, contained an aboriginal population in part Caucasian. The westerly flow of the north equatorial current, together with the easterly trade winds, were such as to make possible fortuitous sailings across the Atlantic and landings in the Caribbean or Gulf of Mexico area. It appears too that the Old World variety of cotton had mixed with that of the Americas before the coming of the Spaniards and that this hybridisation implies human contacts across the Atlantic.

To complete this brief review of the suggested (yet unproven) sources of immigrants into prehistoric America we may glance at the

[1] Thor Heyerdahl, *American Indians in the Pacific* (1952), pp. 595–620.

[2] P. Rivet, *op. cit.*, chap. vi.

[3] Thor Heyerdahl, *op. cit.*, pp. 340–5.

extraordinary suggestion, given the formidable geographical difficulties involved, of a small immigration of Australian aborigines into South America. While physical and social anthropology are alleged to support this view, that derived from the comparative study of languages might appear impressive. It has been found that remarkable affinities—and even identities—exist between more than ninety words in common use among the Australian aborigines on the one hand and Patagonian and Ona Indians on the other.[1] These Indians, who speak the Con language, live south of latitude 42° S. in the extreme south of South America. The geographical aspect of this evidence is itself striking : the affinities relate only to southern South America and are closest with the dialects of eastern Australia. The explanation of the problem thus raised remains obscure. Is it conceivable that Australian aborigines made their way by stages from their homeland across Asia to enter North America in the north-west and then ultimately left cultural traces only in the remote south of South America ? It has been suggested, however, that a sea route between south-east Australia and Cape Horn, making use of intermediate islands as staging points and of coastal waters of Antarctica, might conceivably have been practicable under optimum conditions of post-glacial climate, say around 6,000 years ago. If this hypothesis is ever proved by archaeological discoveries along the line of route, it would then appear that the Americas received intruders in the extreme south comparable with the Eskimos in the extreme north.

It was not North America, today the most economically developed part of the Americas, but certain inter-tropical lands of Middle and South America which first attracted most European interest. It is clear that within these lands many successive cultures, some of which were beyond doubt ' civilised,' had flourished during the thousand years or so before the arrival of the Spaniards. Special interest attaches to those civilisations which still existed at the end of the 15th century —notably the Mayan, Toltec-Aztec, and Incan civilisations—the more so since they grew up in complete or almost complete isolation from those of the Old World. Why were the cultures of certain areas and

[1] See P. Rivet, *op. cit.*, pp. 88–102 (with maps). The remarkable adaptation to cold of the Ona Indians, as also of the Tehuelche Patagonians who, when first seen by Europeans, wore only shoes made from skin, might suggest that their ancestors had endured even greater cold than that of Patagonia and Tierra del Fuego, where the Ona Indians live. But immigrants into Alaska must also have survived extreme cold.

peoples so outstanding, contrasting sharply with modes of life relatively primitive elsewhere ? Did their homelands, by reason of their geographical character, offer any special advantages or stimuli ? Or does the explanation of this high achievement lie in the inner creative forces of certain peoples and thus have little regard to their physical environments ?

The geographical setting of the high civilisations of pre-Columbian America occupied only a small fraction of inter-tropical America. It consisted of the Central American isthmus, the islands, and the South American mainland of the Caribbean Sea, together with Andean lands set between the interior lowlands and the Pacific coast of South America (Fig. 65). Looked at as a whole, these lands comprised a dominant proportion of mountains and highlands and, related to this, as also to the neighbouring seas, a remarkable range of regional and local climates. These were matched by a wide variety of soils, so that in specific sites the physical requirements for cultivation were good and varied. The region has something of the nature of a cross-road location : north-west South America (present-day Colombia) had the most central position with access northwards through the isthmus, southwards towards Peru and beyond, and eastwards across northern Venezuela to the Caribbean islands. A striking geographical advantage of these American inter-tropical lands was their very varied plant life. Indeed, according to Vavilov,[1] they contain two of the eight centres of origin of the world's most important cultivated plants. In this respect the region compares broadly with those Old World centres of origin of cultivated plants, notably in India, China, Indonesia, Ethiopia, the Middle East, and the Mediterranean lands. If the land yielded only a limited fauna, the seas provided a wealth of fish. The most likely place for the beginning of cultivation and animal domestication in the Americas—and perhaps *the* single source of these new arts—is thought by Carl O. Sauer [2] to lie in north-western South America. The principal civilisations when the Spaniards arrived were, however, developed away off to the north and south.

The setting of both Mayan and Toltec-Aztec cultures lies within the isthmian area of Middle America which is flanked by the Atlantic and Pacific oceans (Fig. 65). This isthmus narrows south of Mexico

[1] N. I. Vavilov, *The Origin, Variation, Immunity and Breeding of Cultivated Plants* (Chronica Botanica Co., Massachusetts, 1949–50), pp. 39–44.

[2] Carl O. Sauer, *Agricultural Origins and Dispersals* (American Geographical Society, New York, 1952), p. 42 and Plate II.

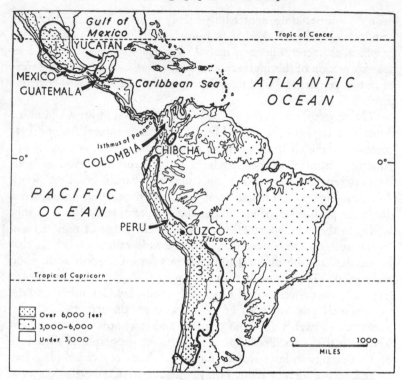

FIG. 65   The location of pre-Columbian civilisations of the Americas.
*Note that the numerals 1, 2 and 3 locate respectively
the Toltec-Aztek, Mayan, and Incan civilisations.*

and its surface stands high and rugged, made up of mountain folds and volcanic masses, except for some lowland stretches along the coasts. As a bridge-land between the continents to the north and south, Central America is geologically young, since it took shape, replacing part of the broad Tethys Sea, only in the latter part of the Tertiary era. To the north the Mexican desert stretches almost from sea to sea, while, southwards of this obstacle, surfaces of high relief and the tropical forests and swamps of the coastlands combine to clog the funnel between North and South America.   Even in these days of engineering triumphs neither modern motor highway nor railway passes through Middle America as a whole to link the United States directly to South America.   Yet it seems virtually certain that peoples migrated through these lands southwards from North America just as during the Pleistocene many animals moved in both directions. The obstacles set by nature were clearly not insuperable to human migrants, for it would appear that climate, in its effects on drainage and vegetation, in some measure eased their movement.

Columbus, and the conquistadores, merchants, and missionaries who followed him, reached that part of the Americas which was then the most populous and the most civilised. This applies less to the coastlands of Venezuela and the West Indian islands, which were occupied scantily and relatively late, chiefly by Arawaks and Caribs, than to specific areas of Middle and South America. Not that these areas were in any sense uniformly well settled then, for, as today, population was markedly clustered in particular tracts. That an estimated three-quarters of the population of the Americas were concentrated in the most civilised parts of Central and South America reflects of course the relatively high population capacity made possible by the advanced sedentary culture of these lands.

Mayan history suggests that their civilisation was somewhat deeply rooted in time. Their ' old empire,' so-called, lasted from the last centuries B.C. until its break-up *c.* A.D. 650 and had its heartland in the tropical lowlands of north and east Guatemala and of eastern Yucatan. It was followed by their ' new empire,' which, located in the somewhat drier area of north-west Yucatan, involved the desertion of their former cities, ruins of which survive. The cause of this migration, which has given rise to much speculation, remains obscure : the impoverishment of the soil by continual cropping and by the leaching effect of heavy rainfall might possibly have been decisive. The older phase of Mayan civilisation reached a higher level of achievement than did the later, which was decadent at the time of Cortez's assault. It, too, has special geographical interest in view of its setting, which is today one of hot and wet tropical forest—no easy environment to confront and to exploit without the aid of iron and steel and mechanical power.

The territorial core in turn of the Toltec and Aztec civilisations was, in contrast, the highlands of south-central Mexico. This area, lying to the south of the Mexican desert, consisted of a number of intermontane basins set within the mountain-girt plateau of Anahuac, beyond which and difficult of access lay wet and wooded coastal lowlands. This base, chiefly because of its high altitude (over 7,000 feet), was less arid than northern Mexico while temperatures, though ranging sharply between day and night, maintained a steady monthly average of 60° F. Whether Toltec denotes a people or is only a geographical term remains in doubt, but it seems that migrants, moving by way of the northern desert, created on the plateau of Anahuac the Toltec empire which flourished from A.D. 600 until A.D. 1100. To these creators of Toltec civilisation is due the name 'Anahuac,' which means 'on the edge of the water.' It referred to the numerous lakes on the floor of the plateau and may well record how this land appealed to immigrants who had crossed the parched desert. The Aztecs moved in along the same route *c.* A.D. 1300 and built their capital at Tenochtitlan, the precursor of Mexico City.

Between Middle America and South America, although peoples must have moved by land as also by rafts and boats, there were no close cultural connections. Difficulties of terrain interposed great obstacles. Beyond the isthmus of Panama, in what is now Colombia, the Andean mountain system, there disposed in three roughly parallel and lofty ranges, dominates the scene, and forests of varying kinds extend widely. Within this vast area the sedentary and civilised Chibcha Indians were established, above all in the intermontane basins of Tunja and Bogota within the eastern cordillera, whence they carried cereals to the coastlands in exchange for salt. The famous Incan civilisation, which characterised the many peoples organised into one empire by the Inca (='king'), extended southwards from the Equator as far as latitude 33° S. It occupied an enormous area—1·2 million square miles, greater than that of the Arabian peninsula—and supported a population estimated at 20 millions. Its geographical pattern is striking: embracing as it did parts of modern Ecuador, Peru, Bolivia, and Chile and bounded westwards by the Pacific, it coincided with the coastlands and the Andean mountain zone, stopping short eastwards near the margin of mountain and plain.

Incan power was based on the cultivated highland basins which, because of their great elevation (10,000 feet or more above sea-level) and despite their latitude, enjoyed temperate climate. And while Incan power extended over the low-lying and largely hot desert coastlands, it was arrested to the east at the forested mountain slopes, below which entirely different environments—those of equatorial forest, scrub prairie, and tropical scrub forest—presented new and vast worlds.

Civilised life in the area occupied by the Incan peoples may go back some thousands of years, but the Incan empire itself was the product of only three centuries before the advent of the Spaniards.

It thus postdates comparable civilisations of Middle America, from which in earlier times cultural currents may have reached it. The capital of the Incan empire lay at Cuzco (latitude 13° S.) in a small basin, standing at 11,000 feet and difficult of access ; tradition placed an earlier homeland farther south on the shores of Lake Titicaca. These places lie in southern Peru, itself a name invented by the Spaniards.

Incan civilisation presents many facets of interest. Its system of government was despotic, yet paternal and efficient. The population was rigidly classified, into nobles of the blood royal, priests, and the peasant masses. A common tongue was imposed—the Quechua language. Religious beliefs and ceremonies centred on the sun as God. The economy was centralised and state-managed and depended on cultivation, especially that of maize and potatoes. The llama and alpaca herds of the mountains were domesticated ; the wild vicuña yielded a fine wool. Cotton had long been grown and was woven. The empire had great wealth of precious metals to which no commercial interest was attached and commanded skills in metal working. Remarkable powers of construction, without the use either of the wheel, or of iron and mechanical power, are demonstrated by the terracing of mountain slopes, the building of aqueducts to bring water down to the desert coastlands, bridges, roads, temples, palaces, and fortresses which defied the firearms of the conquistadores. Yet with all their achievement, which clearly involved intelligent organisation and the heavy toil of the peasant masses, the Incan peoples had not evolved a written language—although knotted string was used to keep records and to convey messages—nor indeed, at the time of Pizarro, had they any clear recollection of their own history.

The civilisations of the Americas cannot of course be simply explained in environmental terms. Certainly their geographical setting enjoyed advantages over such regions as the equatorial forests and the North American interior plains in respect of the great varieties of terrain, soil, climate, plant, and aquatic life, as well as resources of metallic ores and building stone. For Incan agriculture too there were the nitrate fertilisers provided, through the chances of climate,[1] in the off-shore islands of Peru. In short, the bases for civilised living existed

[1] E. G. R. Taylor, *The Haven-finding Art* (1956), pp. 50–1. The accumulation of the guano from sea-birds was dependent on the continuance of specific climatic conditions.

and, according to Nordenskiöld,[1] it was because conditions of life were easy in these inter-tropical lands that they became the locale of Indian inventions and discoveries. Yet life was certainly not easy as a gift of Nature : the lands of Mayan, Aztec, and Incan civilisation were difficult to circulate in and to exploit, especially when it is remembered that, apart from the llama, a relatively poor beast of burden, only human energy was available. So that, in flat contradiction to Nordenskiöld's view, A. J. Toynbee[2] found that the rise of these civilisations illustrated his theory of 'challenge and response' : the Mayan was a successful response to the challenge of the luxuriance of tropical forest ; the Incan a response to two challenges—that of the bleak climate and grudging soil of the plateaux, and also that of the heat and drought of an almost rainless equatorial desert. Environmental conditions were thus at the least permissive, at the most persuasive. What other explanations may be sought ? Does the character of the peoples themselves give any clue to their high achievement ?

This may well appear a hopeless quest. Pittard,[3] however, claimed that, despite the great ethnic variety of the American Indians, one relatively pure race of common ethnic type, characterised by short stature, broad-headedness, projecting cheek-bones, black glossy hair, and prominent noses, was distributed solely in the region between Mexico and Bolivia, which coincides broadly with the first civilised areas of the Americas. Interesting as is this correlation, it does not take us far : ethnic types are somewhat imaginative conceptions and their relationship, if any, to creative ability can only be guessed. Surely the more hopeful answer to our inquiry is found in the history of certain cultivated plants, notably maize and the potato, for it was these, and not the precious stones and metals so dazzling to the Spaniards, which provided the essential basis of the civilisations of Middle and South America.

It is generally agreed that maize or Indian corn (*Zea mays*) originated in the Americas. Early and primitive races of maize were being grown in Mexico as early as 3000–2500 B.C. By 1500 B.C. maize

---

[1] Erland Nordenskiöld, 'The American Indian as an Inventor,' *Jour. Roy. Anth. Inst. of Gt. Britain*, vol. 59 (1929), p. 284. Note his remark cited at the head of this chapter.

[2] A. J. Toynbee, *A Study of History*, abridgement by D. C. Somervell (1946), p. 75.

[3] E. Pittard, *Les Races et l'Histoire* (1924), pp. 554–6.

was being grown on a sufficient scale to affect the way of life. Certainly it had had a long history when Europeans first arrived, for many varieties, distinguished by the colour of the seed, were grown in different areas. The beginning of cultivation at Chilea in Peru may go back as far as 4000 B.C., but maize, together with the art of pottery making, did not reach Peru until about 1500 B.C. This is of interest because maize appears to have derived from a pod corn which grew wild in the savanna lands east of the Andes. It is thus thought originally to have come from South America to Mexico where, by natural crossing with a grass (*Euchlaena Mexicana*), a new variety was created and developed. But whatever the precise history of maize, its importance to the Aztec-Mayan peoples and their civilisation is not in doubt. Its successful cultivation meant the provision of an adequate and storable food supply for sedentary populations and the opportunity for some groups within them to devote themselves to activities other than food-getting and thus to the development of crafts, social organisation, and cultural pursuits.

Similarly it is difficult to conceive of the Incan civilisation but for the potato : without this staple food, its distribution and extent would have been much reduced and its political organisation would have lacked stability. Although many kinds of potato grew wild on the Andean plateaux, in Guatemala, and in Mexico as far north as the Colorado river, actually it was not cultivated outside South America. Its value there as an abundant source of food derived from the successful cultivation of many varieties, including frost-resistant types, on the high Andean plateaux at levels above 11,000–13,000 feet where maize cannot adapt itself to the climate. The antiquity of potato cultivation is eloquently attested by the pottery of successive culture periods, in the decoration of which the potato figures continually, and it can be carried back before the Incan period to at least A.D. 1000. Its main area, the inter-tropical *tierra fria* highlands, stretched from latitude 3° N. to 22° S., and two or even more crops per year could be got from the same plot of land.[1] The art of drying potatoes was early learnt and, as *chuño*, they were carried to areas such as the Peruvian desert where they could not be grown. This valuable food, together with the drug cocaine, derived from the leaf of the coca bush, itself a plant of the high plateaux, were the main supports of that

[1] The potato is the subject of a broadly based, scholarly work : see R. N. Salaman, *The History and Social Influence of the Potato* (1949).

dour and stable peasant population which the Incas so strenuously organised.

American Indians made an important contribution to the world by their independent inventions and discoveries.[1] They contributed a range of cultivated plants which were unknown to the Old World before Columbus : maize, potatoes, sweet potatoes, manioc, cacao, sunflowers, tomatoes, the bottle gourd, and tobacco—to name the chief. Indians in Amazonia learnt how to collect and use rubber, quinine, and the coca drug. Incan Indians too were the first to discover platinum and to weld copper. They were able to make bridges of many kinds— floating, suspension, and cantilever bridges and foot-bridges of poles.

Despite their differences—of technical proficiency, social and political organisation, religious ceremonial, and the like—the Mayan, Aztec, and Incan civilisations reveal many common features. Each was characterised by fixed settlements—villages and towns—and each practised a productive form of agriculture. Skills in fishing in river, lake, and sea were well developed, and the making of sea-going craft and knowledge of seamanship, especially by the Incan peoples, is now known to have been considerable. Viewed as a whole, Indian civilisations are remarkable both for their attainments and for their shortcomings. The Indians could build stone palaces, temples, fortresses, and walls of great strength and decorate them with intricate relief sculptures in stone, ivory, and wood. In areas where stone was lacking, sun-dried bricks were made to provide building material, although on occasions at great effort stone was brought from afar. Agriculture was conducted to a large extent with the aid of elaborate terracing of mountain sides and of irrigation which involved the provision of reservoirs and of water channels. Much skill was acquired in obtaining and working gold, silver, copper, and tin ; bronze was made, and in the Incan Empire a means of gold and silver plating was understood. Similarly the art of road- and bridge-making was sufficiently advanced to make possible the internal circulation necessary for an extensive empire. To these skills should be added the ability to spin and weave cotton and wool and to make and decorate pottery. Finally, the Indian civilisations developed various forms of social and political organisation, whilst in the field of mathematics the Mayas in particular achieved much—witness their very accurate calendar and their understanding of decimals.

[1] Erland Nordenskiöld, *op. cit.*, pp. 273–309.

In contrast, these civilisations, compared with those much earlier developed in the riverine lands of the Old World, showed some conspicuous deficiencies. They appear to have possessed no alphabets, although some Mayan hieroglyphic writing (codices and inscriptions) has survived, and the Incans could communicate by the use of knotted threads. They appear, too, not to have worked iron nor possessed iron implements. They did not understand how to construct a storeyed building or the keystone arch or to use the wheel for transport and pottery-making. They had few domesticated animals save the dog, poultry, including the musk duck, the turkey of Mexico, and the llama and alpaca in the Andean highlands. They did not grow wheat, rice, barley, or rye. And the practices of human sacrifices to propitiate many gods and also cannibalism still persisted.

The historical geography of the Indians of North America during the thousands of years which elapsed before the coming of the first Europeans can be seen only dimly. Strictly speaking, they had no history, since they left no written records, not even inscriptions. The task of reconstructing their story devolves on the archaeologist who has, however, the rare advantage of ' catching some of his archaeology alive,' since in small numbers they survive. While this work has far yet to go, finds, indicating man's early presence 10,000 or more years ago, have been made widely in the areas south of those covered by Pleistocene ice sheets. Human remains and artefacts are found in association with fauna characteristic of Europe during the Great Ice Age. Carbon[14] dating, however, indicates how much longer such animals survived in North America, in part as a result of man's late advent and small numbers. The archaeological record depicts at first nomadic or semi-nomadic food-collectors and hunters, armed with weapons of stone, hunting big game—mastodons, mammoths, bison, and the American camel—while the presence of a small variety of horse, which was also hunted, is well attested by its bones.

It is of great interest to note the very different values which attached to major parts of the North American area, values so markedly different from those which they now possess. What has been roundly called the Greater South-western Area, which includes the present states of New Mexico, Arizona, Nevada, Utah, and the south-western half of Colorado, occupies a place in Indian history in inverse proportion to its present importance in the United States. The physical geographer now relates this extensive area, which lay outside the limits of glaciation, to the Basin and Range Province and the Colorado

Plateau. It is made up physically of block mountains, basins of internal drainage, and the Colorado Plateau, barrier-like because of the canyons which incise its surface and largely reduced to sheer desert by heat and low rainfall. Today the arid south-west is, except for Alaska, the least populated major region of the United States, redeemed somewhat by its mineral wealth—gold, silver, and copper—and by some large-scale irrigation works. Yet during the Indian phase it reveals the earliest cultures, notably those associated with Sandia, Fulsom, and Clovis, New Mexico, and with Cochise, Arizona. Until the close of the Mankato phase of the Wisconsin glaciation, the region appears to have been well watered. The stone artefacts, Upper Palaeolithic in type, are found beneath water-borne deposits ; high-level sites—terraces and morainic hills—appear to have been preferred.

From the beginning of the Christian era a succession of distinct cultures reveals unmistakable advances in the material culture of the south-west : cliff houses, villages, and eventually towns (*pueblos*) ; basket-making, weaving, and later pottery-making ; the cultivation of the soil for maize and pumpkins with the aid of digging-sticks ; the bow and arrow, developed from the spear-thrower ; and the advent of the turkey. A certain amount of long-distance trade—despite the absence of wheeled vehicles and beasts of burden—was clearly undertaken by some of the Indian tribes from Arizona : shells were brought there from the Pacific coast in return for textiles, and salt from the Colorado river. The proximity of the south-west to Mexico and to the Caribbean world clearly explains in part its cultural ascendancy in North America. It would seem to have become the primary centre from which new techniques, notably maize-growing, were diffused as far afield as the Atlantic coastlands. Abandoned Indian fields are reported there during the initial period of European settlement.[1]

[1] Ralph H. Brown, *Historical Geography of the United States* (1948), pp. 12–19.

CHAPTER XI

Europe and China

We alone possess two eyes, the Europeans are one-eyed, and all the other inhabitants of the earth are blind.

Chinese proverb

EVEN today, when distance has been almost annihilated by new means of communication and transport, and the separateness of East and West no longer exists, we tend to think of Europe and China, notwithstanding their political, linguistic, and other divisions, as two homelands of distinct and unrelated cultural traditions. Until recent times Europe and China formed separate worlds and, like Kipling's cat, each walked by itself. Largely independent in their development and largely aloof from each other, Europe and China derived their civilisations from different sources at about the same time. Whereas the former owes much to the Ægean world and in particular to ancient Greece, the latter evolved its earliest civilisation on the bordering lands of the Hoang-ho or Yellow River during the last three millennia B.C. Whereas Europe became Christian, China adopted Indian Buddhism together with the ethical ideas of its native Confucius. The historically recent impact of 'Western Civilisation' on China, which reached it directly from Europe and indirectly from the United States and from Japan, is only now drastically modifying Chinese ways of life and thought.

It is a nice question, which archaeological research may ultimately answer, to what extent, in their earliest stages, Chinese and European civilisations received practices and ideas from a common source, notably from the lands of earliest civilisation in western Asia and Egypt.[1] It is believed that the knowledge of agriculture, of the potter's art, and of the use of copper reached northern China, by way of Central Asia, either from Russian Turkestan or from Persia, as early as about

[1] See above, Chapter IX.

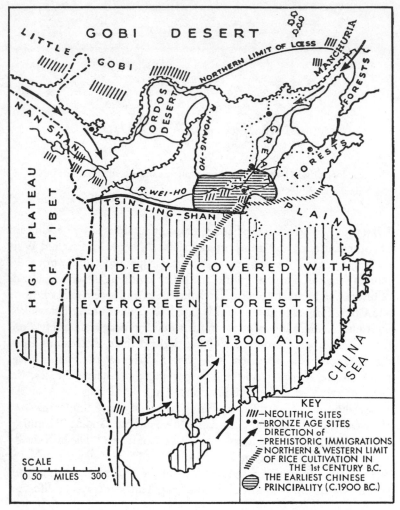

FIG. 66   A composite historical map of China.

3000 or 2500 B.C.   If this is so, we may say that the initial, or Neolithic, civilisation of China came indirectly from the ancient centres in western Asia—from either the lower Indus lands or from Lower Mesopotamia, areas from which cultural currents equally passed into Europe.   Subsequently to this remote phase, however, Chinese civilisation seems to have developed in almost complete independence of influences from the West.

Chinese civilisation was born in the valleys and plateaux of north China through which the great river Hoang-ho flows in a steeply-sided valley. North China is bordered northwards by the steppes and deserts of Gobi and by the forests of southern Manchuria ; on the east by the sea ; and on the west and south by the mountain ranges of Nan-Shan and Tsin-Ling-Shan respectively (Fig. 66). Thick deposits of loess, together with river alluvium, cover a great part of this area. The loess of north China is a fine-grained silt which was carried there by westerly winds from the neighbouring deserts. It gave rise to ' Yellow Earth,' rich in plant foods, easy to work, and free of dense vegetation. Since the annual rainfall of north China averages less than thirty inches and, moreover, is very variable from year to year, sufficient moisture for cultivation was not always available, and recurrent drought, together with river floods, resulted in continual and disastrous famines. The earliest settlers in north China, those of the Neolithic period, occupied areas where rainfall is now as low as ten inches a year. They already worked the soil with a hoe and maintained its fertility by simple irrigation methods. It is significant geographically that both Neolithic and, subsequently, Bronze Age, settlements avoided the Great Plain through which, in ever changing channels, the Hoang-ho made its way to the sea. The lower Hoang-ho—' China's Sorrow,' the river is called—is subject to violent floods in spring, and great organised efforts were necessary, not only to embank its waters but also to convert to agricultural uses the jungles and swamps which originally covered much of the Great Plain.

The earliest known Chinese principality, which formed the nucleus around which Chinese civilisation spread, extended across the Hoang-ho valley into the western margin of the Great Plain (Fig. 66). The geographical heartland of China under the Han dynasty (206 B.C. to A.D. 220) was the loess-floored valley of the Wei-ho, a tributary of the Hoang-ho, along which passed the route westwards to the Tarim Basin (Chinese Turkestan). This was the base from which the Chinese conquered and civilised the peoples of central and southern China, which were well-wooded lands, climatically well fitted for cultivation. In this region, rice, which is believed to have been native there, was the chief grain crop ; in north China millet and wheat were the staple crops (Fig. 66). It was the emperors of the Han dynasty who carried Chinese civilisation across the Yangtse river to the coastlands and to the mountainous border of Annam (modern Vietnam, Cambodia, and Laos).

In the 1st century A.D. two highly developed and distinct civilisations were established on the western and eastern margins of Eurasia (Fig. 67). In the west, flanked by the then impassable Atlantic, stood the Roman Empire, the axis of which was the Mediterranean 'lake.' In the east, beyond which stretched the vast Pacific, stood the Chinese states, which, however divided politically, shared a common culture. Both the Roman Empire and China occupied warm temperate latitudes, but whereas the former extended into cool temperate lands, the latter stretched into the tropics ; both, too, were extended longitudinally. Actually, the western extension of China, between long. 120°

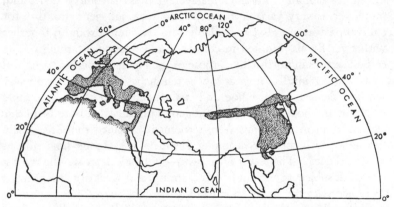

FIG. 67   The Roman Empire and China in the
1st century A.D.

and 70° E., represented conquered lands in the steppe of Central Asia, where the nomadic way of life prevailed. Further, the two empires were equally populous : a census of A.D. 156 estimated the Chinese population at over fifty millions ; compare the figure of 70 millions estimated by scholars for the population of the Roman Empire.[1] The simplified rainfall map (Fig. 60, p. 130) suggests that both Europe and China stood at the terminals of a steppe-desert belt where rainfall was sufficient for cultivation ; hence they were geographically equipped to support relatively dense sedentary populations. But it should be remembered that in north China, as also in parts of the Roman Empire, resort to irrigation was often desirable or even necessary for the purposes of agriculture.

[1] So also the populations of China and Europe today are roughly equal : the former has about 700 millions, the latter about 600 millions.

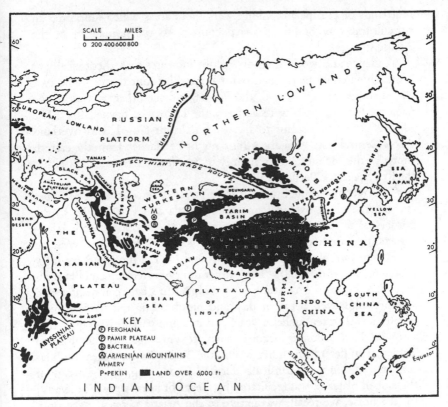

Fig. 68 The major physical divisions of Asia.
The Scythian caravan route is shown.

Why did Europe and China develop along independent lines, and why were they so largely insulated from each other? Certainly geographical conditions answer this question. Sheer distance itself was an obstacle to their interrelations, the more so when we recall the means of transport formerly available—the caravan by land and the sailing ship by sea. Moreover, a broad continental area of mountains, steppe, and desert, which was bordered northwards by vast forests and marshy tracts, lay interposed in Central Asia between Europe and China, which had well-watered plains, plateaux, and river valleys, occupied by settled agriculturalists (Fig. 20, p. 46). Although the landward limits of Europe and China at different periods of history are somewhat difficult to discover, there is no doubt that the essential heartlands of Europe and China were those areas which supported an agricultural way of life in sharp contrast to the nomadism of the Asiatic steppes.

A glance at a world map or a globe indicates that, theoretically at least, China could be reached from Europe by four routes. The two all-sea routes, one by way of the Pacific, and the other by way of the Cape of Good Hope, were actually the last to be opened up. The third route, which seems to have been the first used, was overland across Central Asia. Finally, China might be reached from the eastern shores of the Mediterranean, mainly by sea, if use were made of either the Red Sea or the Persian Gulf.

The overland route involved long passages across the high steppes and deserts which extend from south Russia and Persia as far as the borders of north China. The steppes and deserts of Central Asia— for example, those of Gobi, Djungaria, the Tarim Basin, and Western Turkestan—are high plateaux, girt around for the most part by lofty mountain chains (Fig. 68). They suffer not only freezing and blizzards in winter but also great ranges of temperature between winter and summer, and even between day and night. The rainfall is scanty, usually less than ten inches a year, and in some parts it is so little that virtually lifeless deserts occur ; such, for example, is the dreaded Taklamakan desert which lies within the Tarim Basin, a great undulating area of arid yet intrinsically fertile ' sands ' (Fig. 69). Passage of these open plateaux was facilitated by means of horse-drawn caravans ; for the horse, we recall, was native to the Asiatic steppes. Not only had caravans to cross wide spaces alternately scorched and frozen, they had also to traverse the mountain obstacles which lay across their path. From the high, dissected plateau of Pamir, mountain chains diverge in almost all directions—the Hindu Kush, the Himalayas, the Altyn Tagh, the Kunlun, the Tien-Shan, and the Altai, to name the chief (Fig. 68). At the foot of mountains, where they adjoin the plateaux, towns such as Samarkand, Kashgar, and Khotan arose as convenient halts on the overland routes [1] (Fig. 69). But it is necessary to emphasise that the physical obstacles to passage across Central Asia were insufficient to deter merchants, if opportunities for trade existed ; in fact—as we have argued elsewhere—this vast area facilitated transportation. The chief obstacle to the use of this route was human rather than physical. The political divisions and rivalries of the nomad peoples of Central

[1] See above, Chapter VI, p. 91.

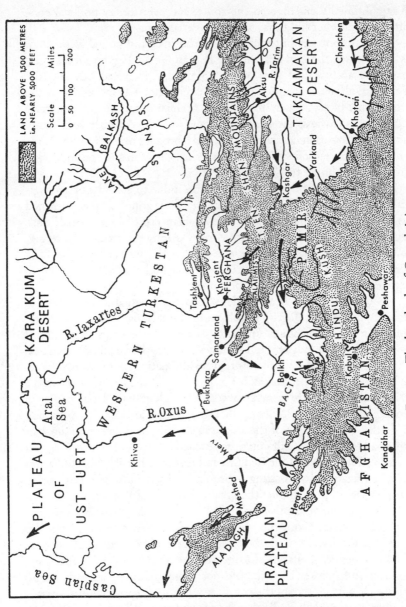

Fig. 69 The heartlands of Central Asia.

The arrows indicate the medieval routes from China to the West.

Asia continually endangered the route, and even today political conditions of another kind may impede overland travel.

More important historically than the overland route were those which utilised the Red Sea and the Persian Gulf. Fig. 70 shows what has been aptly called the 'waist' of Asia. The Red Sea and the Persian Gulf wash the western and eastern shores respectively of the rigid crust-block which forms the Arabian plateau and penetrate northwards towards the Mediterranean from the Arabian Sea. Only a narrow isthmus in northern Egypt and a broader one in Mesopotamia and Syria prevent direct intercourse by sea between Europe and India, the half-way house to China.

The existence of these two water arms is due to episodes of geological history. The Red Sea constitutes a 'fault zone' : it was formed as a result of the shattering of the Arabian crust-block, which once extended unbroken into northern Africa. Along the zone of shattering, subsidence took place and the sea entered the sunken trough. The Persian Gulf, in contrast, is part of a great ' sunkland ' or trough which extends northwards into Mesopotamia.

The valley of the lower Nile, which was navigable, and those of the Euphrates and Tigris, which were scarcely navigable up-stream, maintain the north-south direction of the Red Sea and Persian Gulf respectively, and indicate land passages towards the Mediterranean Sea. Across the waist of Asia, therefore, two alternative routes were offered. The one which passed through Egypt involved the use of boats on the Nile and a passage by caravan across the high eastern desert of Egypt to the Red Sea ports. The other led from the ports of Syria and Palestine to the valley of the Euphrates or Tigris, whence by boat or by road the Persian Gulf could be reached.

From the outlet of the Red Sea and from the Persian Gulf India was reached at first by coasting. Similarly, by a number of coasting voyages from port to port the products of China were brought westwards by seamen familiar with different stretches of the coasts and waters. When, about the year A.D. 50, the Greek seaman Hippalus used the south-west monsoon to steer a direct course from the Persian Gulf to western India, he showed that sea routes might be followed, shorter and quicker than the old coastwise sailings. Since the monsoons blow from the south-west in summer and from the north-east in winter, they could be utilised both for outward and homeward voyages.

Each sea had its own physical peculiarities in respect of winds, channels, coasts, and harbours. Thus, in the Red Sea, where northerly

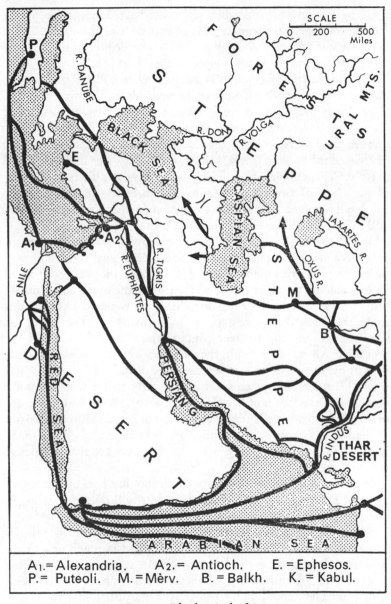

FIG. 70 The 'waist' of Asia.
Roman routes are shown.

winds were prevalent and where the coasts were inhospitable, much local knowledge was necessary to navigators. The Strait of Malacca, between Sumatra and the Malay peninsula, afforded the usual and most direct access from the Indian Ocean to the China Sea.

It is not certain whether, as Herodotus related, Phoenician seamen circumnavigated Africa from east to west about the year 600 B.C. Even if they did, their enterprise bore no results. The opening-up of the oceanic route from Europe to India, the East Indies, and China, awaited the discoveries of Portuguese navigators. Bartholomew Diaz discovered the Cape of Good Hope in 1494, and Vasco da Gama sailed as far as Calicut in western India in 1498. Why was the route by way of the Cape of Good Hope discovered so late ? In part at least, because it involved very serious navigational difficulties in the days of sail. The west African coast in tropical latitudes is barren and inhospitable ; moreover, north of the Equator ships had to pass through an area of calms—'the doldrums'—which long proved forbidding and called for both great courage and skill. Further, it was necessary to understand and to utilise the wind systems to the north and south of this obstacle. Actually, when merchantmen came to frequent this route, they learned to make good use of the many island groups of the southern Atlantic and to steer courses which made best use of the prevailing winds. As a result, their courses were by no means coast-wise or direct : in order to take advantage of the north-east winds in tropical latitudes ships steered a south-westerly course which brought them towards the coasts of Brazil (Fig. 12, p. 30). Some East Indiamen, *en route* for India, actually touched the coast of Brazil at Rio de Janeiro ! In the Indian Ocean and the China Sea ships depended on the monsoons, and the times of sailing were closely adapted to their periodical occurrence.

We have indicated above what were the possible lines of intercourse between Europe and China ; let us now briefly sketch some stages in the history of their interrelations.

It has already been suggested that archaeological evidence shows that ideas and practices reached China overland in prehistoric times. At a much later time, in the 6th century B.C., some highly specialised ' socked celts ' (bronze axes), which in much earlier times had been widely used in central and south-eastern Europe, found their way overland to China. Rather later, about the year 450 B.C., the existence of China is recorded for the first time in European literature. According to Herodotus, a Greek named Aristeas, in the 6th or 7th century B.C.,

claimed to have journeyed across Central Asia as far as the Djungarian
Basin and the Altai mountains (see Fig. 68). There he heard of the
Chinese as a settled and prosperous people who dwelt by a never-frozen
sea. A legend recorded in the time of Herodotus described the
Chinese as 'vegetarians'; this is not without geographical interest,
since it emphasises their distinctness, as cultivators living on grain, from
the nomadic peoples of the steppe, who lived on meat and milk. In
Herodotus' day, too, the Scythians, themselves Asiatic nomads who
were established on the south Russian plain westwards of the lower
Don, traded by caravan with Asiatic peoples as far east as the Altai
mountains (Fig. 68). Caravans started from the Greek city of Tanais,
which stood at the mouth of the Don ; they passed southwards of, not
across, the Ural mountains, thus using the broad Ural–Caspian Gate.
In the course of their trade along this route the Scythians needed
interpreters of seven languages—so many different peoples occupied
the land. At the end of their journey they probably exchanged metal
goods, horse-trappings, and rugs in return for gold, derived from the
south-eastern side of the Altai.

The caravan route of the Scythians, owing to political disturbances
in Asia, was closed soon after 400 B.C., and later Greek geographers
retained little knowledge of the country through which it had passed.
They even forgot that the Caspian was an enclosed sea ! Nor does it
appear that the Persian Empire entered into relation with China at this
time, although its territories extended to the Aral Sea and included
western Turkestan. When, in 329 B.C., Alexander the Great over-
threw the Persian Empire and advanced into Bukhara and southern
Turkestan, he did not attempt further conquests in Central Asia. Not
without good reason, for beyond the oases of Merv, Bukhara, and
Samarkand, where agriculture and fixed settlements were established,
stretched deterrent lands—an alien world of open steppe above which
rose the lofty ramparts of the Hindu Kush and the Tien-Shan (see
Fig. 69). Alexander founded some military and civil centres, such as
Khojent on the Iaxartes river, but these outliers of Greek culture in
Asia were soon abandoned to a conquering nomadic people, the
Yue-chi.

What efforts were made by China itself to establish relations with
the West ? In the year 128 B.C. the Emperor Wu Ti, of the Han
dynasty, sent an embassy to the Yue-chi, whose court lay near Bukhara.
This embassy—which eventually reached Ferghana, Bukhara, and
Bactria (see Fig. 69)—had important results. It provided China with

the geographical knowledge on which it based an imperialistic policy in Central Asia. It led also to the introduction into China of the vine, which the Greeks had brought into Bukhara and Samarkand. The Chinese policy of western expansion proved successful. By defeating the Huns, a powerful nomad people who occupied Mongolia, China extended its dominion as far west as the oases of Ferghana. It sent embassies to Parthia and Bukhara, and some exchanges were made of gold and silk, then unknown in the west, for their local products, especially the coveted horses of Ferghana. The Chinese themselves, therefore, as a result of their imperialism, came into contact with west Asian peoples who dwelt beyond the mountain–desert divide of the Tarim Basin, the Tien-Shan and the Hindu Kush.

The knowledge and use of silk spread into the Græco-Roman world during the 1st century B.C. from Parthia, a strong and independent state which occupied the Iranian plateau and was thus well placed to become an intermediary between China and the Mediterranean lands. The silk route from China passed along the northern foot of the Nan-Shan and Altyn Tagh mountains to Lop Nor ; thence it continued across the Tarim Basin (Chinese Turkestan) to Kashgar, keeping along either the northern or the southern flank of the Taklamakan desert ; finally, it crossed the high Pamir plateau into the oases of Ferghana, and passed through Merv into Parthia (Fig. 69, p. 169).

A flourishing trade between the Roman Empire and China, which reached its height in the 2nd century A.D., was established less by means of the overland route through Parthia than by the use of the sea routes, especially that which led to Egypt (Fig. 70). Silk was the first among many products sought from China, and its importation on an increasing scale was effected with the aid of intermediaries—Arabs, Indians, Parthians, and Chinese. Roman citizens themselves, in particular Greeks, Syrians, and Jews, controlled directly only the western part of the routes. It was the supremacy of Rome in the Mediterranean, in Egypt, and in the Red Sea, towards the end of the 1st century B.C., which provided political conditions favourable to the growth of trade with the East, particularly by the Egypt–Red Sea route. Rome did not open up this route for the first time ; the Ptolemaic rulers of Egypt had already used it. With the aid of the monsoons, however, which speeded up the voyage between the Gulf of Aden and India, the Egyptian route acquired a new importance. The ports of peninsular India offered the Roman world not only their own local products, such as spices, cottons, gems, and gold, but also Chinese silks, pearls, and drugs, which reached them by diverse routes, either directly by sea, or overland by long and difficult routes ; across the Khyber Pass to the Indus valley ; via Tibet and Sikkim to Patna and thence to the Ganges delta ; and even through Burma and Siam to the ports at the mouths of the Irrawaddy and Salwen rivers.

In the towns of Egypt and Syria, especially at Alexandria and Antioch, which stood at terminals of the sea routes, silk goods were finished off or remade for the Roman market.

In the 2nd century A.D. some Roman sailors actually reached China directly by sea, by rounding Cape Comorin in southern India and passing through the Strait of Malacca. They used the south-west monsoon to carry them into the South China Sea, and landed at Hanoi in Tongking, which was then part of China. But the seaway between India and China, familiar and frequented as it was by Chinese junks and Indian dhows, was not used to forge direct links between Rome and China ; no official embassy seems to have reached Rome from China or vice versa, although by China one attempt to establish diplomatic relations was made.

During and after the 3rd century A.D., when the power of Rome was declining, its indirect trade relations with China weakened. The Abyssinian kingdom of Axum cut the Red Sea route by its conquest of lands on either side of the Strait of Bab-el-Mandeb and the Gulf of Aden, so that it was able to control the Red Sea ' gate ' (see Fig. 70). The silk trade passed into the control of the Abyssinians and the Persians, who, in A.D. 224, inherited by right of conquest the Parthian Empire. Silk continued to reach Syria by the overland route via Kashgar, and when, in A.D. 330, the capital of the Roman Empire was moved to Constantinople, that city became another terminus of the overland route. Early in the 6th century, as a result of a trade agreement between Persia and Axum, the former was able to create a monopoly of the silk trade ; prices rose steeply in the Roman market, but the situation was eased dramatically by the introduction of silk-moth eggs into Europe for the first time. About the year A.D. 552, some eggs of the Chinese silk moth *Bombyx mori*, hidden in a bamboo cane, were brought to Constantinople. The closely guarded secret of sericulture, which China had so long and profitably exploited, thus reached Europe, and the rearing of the silk moth was successfully undertaken in the Roman lands of Syria and southern Greece.[1] The

[1] See above, Chapter VIII, p. 127.

Chinese monopoly in silk production was therefore undermined. With the rapid increase of silk production in Syria and Greece, the Roman Empire became largely independent of Chinese supplies, and the workshops of Constantinople, which became famous for their luxurious silken fabrics, including the imperial 'purple' itself, had a sufficient local supply of raw material.

For some six centuries after the 6th century A.D., Christian Europe virtually broke off intercourse with China, about which it knew and

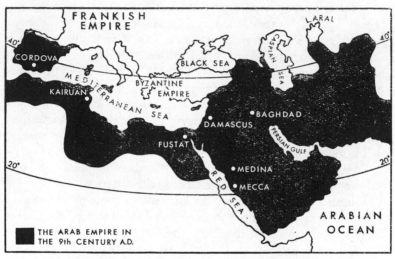

FIG. 71   The Arab Empire at its maximum extent.
Note that this extensive land area lay astride most
of the routes between Europe and the Far East.

remembered little.   There are many reasons to account for this. Political conditions were disturbed alike in Europe, China, and western and central Asia, and Europe had silk supplies of its own, especially from Greece.   Moreover, the Arab Caliphate, which reached its maximum extent in the 8th century, stood interposed, as a hostile and 'infidel' power, between Europe and the Far East, for its territories in Persia, Egypt, and Syria and around the Aral Sea stood astride most of the routes to the Far East (see Fig. 71).   The Seljuk Turks, too, a warlike nomadic people, held sway during part of this period over large areas of central and western Asia.

The creation in the 13th century of the vast Mongol Empire, which is associated with the name and family of Genghiz Khan, made possible direct overland communication with China. From their homeland on the Mongolian steppes, the Mongol horsemen conquered more extensively than the Chinese had ever done. China itself, together with Korea, Central Asia, Persia, and even Russia, fell under their control (Fig. 72). Europe itself was threatened by Mongol armies which advanced into Poland, Hungary, and Silesia, but they did not succeed in permanently holding these marginal lands, and effectively their empire ended at the western terminals of the Eurasian steppe belt. The great Khanate, as the Mongol Empire was called, depended for its unity on horse-riding and the horse caravan as means of communication and transport. Although it was divided into a number of khanates, ruled in turn by sons and grandsons of Genghiz Khan, the overlordship of the Great Khan was generally admitted, so that order and security were established from the coast of the Pacific to those of the Black Sea and the Persian Gulf. China, with its dense population, its agricultural wealth, and its numerous cities and seaports, formed the heartland of the Mongol Empire, and (in 1264) the capital was moved from Mongolia to Peking and Xanadu, which became respectively the winter and summer seats of the Great Khan and his court.

As a result of the Mongol supremacy, a new chapter began in the story of Europe's relations with China. Much use was made of overland routes as well as of the sea route to the Persian Gulf (Fig. 72). During the 13th century the Venetians and Genoese in turn established trading stations in the Crimean peninsula at western terminals of the overland route. In this century, too, the Venetian merchants Nicolo and Maffeo Polo made their overland journey to Peking, and when, between 1271 and 1275, they returned to the court of the Great Khan, Marco Polo, the son of Nicolo, accompanied them. Marco Polo's famous account of Central Asia and China, which was based on seventeen years' sojourn there in the service of the Great Khan, described graphically and almost unbelievably to Europeans the splendour and quality of Chinese civilisation, although it is well to remember that for some three centuries before Marco Polo's *Travels* appeared, the Moslem world, in contrast to the Christian, possessed detailed accounts of China and Central Asia. In the 14th century Christian missions were established at Peking and at Zayton (near Amoy) in south China, where Genoese merchants are known to have resided.

In short, Europe rediscovered China, the Seres of antiquity, which they now knew as Cathay. The silk trade revived ; finished fabrics rather than raw silk were imported. China, it would seem, made

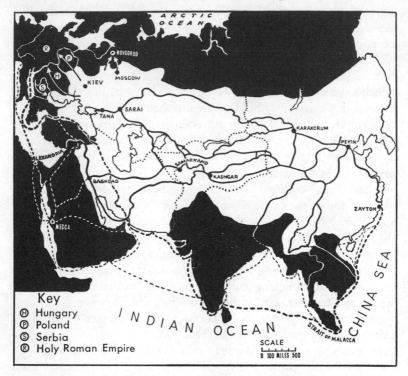

Fig. 72   The routes between Europe and China and the extent
of the Mongol Empire (left white), *c.* A.D. 1290.

technical contributions to Europe ; the making of paper from rags
reached Europe from China via the Arab world, whilst it is possible
that Germany received from Korea the invention of movable type,[1]
which made practicable in the mid-15th century the printing of books
on a large scale.

One final phase, we may note, in the long story of the intermittent
and slender relations between Europe and China—the discovery of the
oceanic routes to Cathay. The stimulus to this maritime enterprise
was at least in part economic—the Portuguese desire to challenge the
monopoly in the eastern trade which was enjoyed by Venice and Genoa.
The closure of one of the old routes to China, owing to the capture of
Constantinople in 1453 by the Ottoman Turks, provided an additional

[1] For a discussion of this unsettled problem, see G. F. Hudson, *Europe and
China* (1931), pp. 165-8.

motive for the discovery of new routes. In 1514, after they had defeated the Arabs in the Indian Ocean and captured Malacca, the Portuguese sailed thence to China. Later they were allowed to settle in Kwangtung at Macao, at the mouth of the Canton river, which eventually became, as it still remains, a Portuguese possession. Dutch, English, and others sought trade in Chinese goods, either directly at Chinese ports or at intermediate places in Malay and Indo-China. Silk goods, the drug rhubarb, porcelain, lacquer work, and, especially in the 18th century, tea formed the chief products sought from China. Yet another route to China lay unexplored—that across the great expanse of the Pacific Ocean. Magellan's ship, which circumnavigated the world in the service of Spain between 1519 and 1522, reached, by way of the Pacific, the Philippine Islands on the threshold of the Chinese world. In 1571 a Spanish fleet crossed the Pacific from Mexico and seized Manila in the Philippine Islands. In thus opening up a new sea route to the Far East by a voyage westwards, Spain succeeded in achieving the purpose which had baffled Christopher Columbus.

CHAPTER XII

International Politics

We speak sometimes of our epoch as the continental era.
MAXIMILIEN SORRE, *L'Homme sur la Terre*

THERE is a geography behind international politics today no less than behind those of the past, the study of which falls to the historian. It is evident that political decisions, plans, situations, and problems cannot be divorced from those finite and specific considerations of environment which the geographer is concerned to assess. International politics arise out of the fact that the surface of the earth is divided—very unequally from place to place—into political units or states, most of which are nowadays independent or sovereign. These states, while enjoying equality of status in international law and (with few exceptions) [1] entitlement to equal membership of the United Nations Organisation, are otherwise remarkably different in many respects—in location, area, population numbers and trends, political organisation, nationality, language, and economic and cultural levels. So also do they differ sharply in their specific attitudes, aspirations, military strength, stages of development, and political stature. Inevitably states have relations, more or less close and friendly, with each other, both locally and at long range. Since for most states territorial contiguity is the norm—New Zealand and Iceland, for example, are exceptional in having no land frontiers—at the least states are involved in frontier control *vis-à-vis* their immediate neighbours. But a variety of interests involve them with each other at long remove, ever more closely as transport and communication become more rapid and efficient.

[1] Independent states of miniature scale, such as Liechtenstein, are deemed ineligible to become U.N. members since they lack the resources needed to share the responsibilities of membership. Switzerland, the better to preserve its neutral status, has never sought membership, while the Chinese People's Republic has failed to obtain it.

The relations between states, which constitute the external aspect of their activities, necessarily relate to a wide range of matters where their several interests and purposes may be in conflict. Such are matters pertaining to political aims, defensive needs, and commercial and cultural objectives. Certainly over a wide field of interests— so-called 'technical' issues, such as transport and postal services— states co-operate smoothly and efficiently. But each state seeks above all else to increase its own economic well-being and to ensure its security and survival—no easy objectives to attain in a world where, despite the great and unparalleled opportunities opened up by modern science and technology, internal and external dangers underline the need for awareness and caution in state policy. Among those who become as it were historians of the present, seeking to explain the complex problems of the contemporary international scene, are political geographers so-called, for whom states and combinations of states are the natural regions for investigation.

From the geographer's standpoint, and using his knowledge and method, the political geographer focuses his attention on the political world of today. The states, for the most part 'nation states,' which pattern the continents, are separate groups of mankind, each organised politically within its own territory and in a particular location. States are thus, among other things, geographical phenomena, indeed 'regions.' Their territories, made up of land and in most cases also of a zone of peripheral sea, are geographically different in many ways, as also are the communities which inhabit them. States therefore can be studied geographically with profit. Such study throws light on their relative degrees of coherence, manpower, economic strength, defence capability, and viability.

It is obvious that at least an elementary knowledge of geography is necessary to understand the news from overseas which finds its place in our newspapers and periodicals. As Sir Halford Mackinder noted over fifty years ago, the world has become such a delicate interlocking mechanism that events at one point can cause repercussions widely and remotely. We are faced with unceasing reports of local events and situations which may quickly acquire international interest and importance. These often occur in places remote and little known, at least to everyman. The spotlight shifts from continent to continent. Since World War II ended, dangerous international situations, which evoked vigorous or violent action or even war, have arisen to claim world-wide attention in many places, notably Berlin, Korea, Suez, Hungary,

Laos, and Cuba. Although a laborious and searching analysis would be necessary in each case to explain these international situations, clearly locational facts must first be grasped. Thus Western Berlin, in Allied military occupation, lies as an 'international exclave' within the territory of Eastern Germany, the German Democratic Republic, itself a satellite of the U.S.S.R. Korea occupies a peninsular territory in the Far East, where the two great land-based Communist states meet the sea power of the United States along a narrow front. ' Suez ' in the present context stands for the isthmus in Egypt which is crossed by both the inter-oceanic canal and the land route from lower Egypt to Palestine. Hungary, lying adjacent to Soviet Ukraine, is a lowland, landlocked country from which routes lie open towards Western, Central, and Mediterranean Europe. Laos, a newly emerged and inland state, occupies a buffer position between, on the one hand, mainland China and its satellite North Vietnam and, on the other, that part of the world which is variously styled ' Western,' ' Oceanic,' ' Free,' and ' Anti-Communist.' Lastly, the island republic of Cuba, reckoned by American geographers to be part of North, rather than Central, America, lies near to Florida in the United States and athwart its routes to and from the Panama Canal. In each of these theatres of international tension or conflict, location was clearly one among the factors of geopolitical significance, and mere reference to an atlas and a globe helps us to begin to understand why so much international concern and tension were generated there.

But it may be fairly claimed that geographical analysis can offer more towards the understanding of international politics than just an appreciation of the facts of location. The geographical method, applied to particular case studies, can throw into relief a whole range of considerations, related in place, which have some bearing on the status, strength, behaviour, and relations of states. The nature of the state territory—in respect of its scale, climate, relief, soils, vegetation cover, and mineral resources—will bear a certain relation to its stature and policies, although these are modified, it is true, by the cultural effort which has been applied to it. The population of the state, both in its quantitative and qualitative aspects, no less repays analysis. What is the population total, what is its rate of growth, and what is its age-distribution, which clearly governs the manpower available for the economy and the armed forces ? The geographical distribution of the population, and the way in which it is settled in towns of differing size and in villages and farms, are also not without political relevance :

witness, for example, how in Malaya in order to counter Communist guerrilla operations it was found expedient to resettle the population of some areas in fortifiable villages. Similarly analysis of the economic geography of the state indicates the nature and scale of industrial and agricultural effort, the degree to which it is self-sufficient in foodstuffs, raw materials, sources of energy, and manufactures. It would indicate further the nature of a state's dependence for essential supplies on others, either close at hand or far off.

There are many other aspects of the state which need to be examined before it is possible to conceive it, in a particular case, as a regional reality—rather than as a shadowy and perhaps emotive image. Among these let us note the historical aspect, the study of which illuminates political attitudes and policies, even though it may little enable us to predict. Such study could hardly have enabled us to foresee, for example, that, after almost a century of conflict, including three wars, the governments of France and (Western) Germany would, following the Treaty of Rome (1957), sign another treaty in 1963 providing for the means closely to align their foreign, military, and cultural policies. On the other hand, episodes of national history are not easily forgotten and their recollection may well have some relevance to current attitudes and decisions. Was not the United States attitude towards Cuba strongly coloured by the fact that it was for several decades after 1898 an American dependency? Is it not also related to the Monroe Doctrine, which for over a century has sought to warn off European states from interfering politically in the republics of the Americas? Is the Mongol phase of Russian history wholly forgotten by the rulers of the Kremlin when confronted with the difficulty of reconciling their foreign policy with that of their Chinese ally? Does Polish co-operation with the U.S.S.R. obliterate the effects of a long tradition of Russo-Polish antagonism?

In other respects, too, forces generated in the historical past activate international politics today. Outworn though it appears to some, novel and exhilarating to others, the political force of nationalism has still widely to be reckoned with, even though some nations have largely outgrown it, and even by Communists who once hoped, and hope ultimately, to replace it by a wider loyalty between working men everywhere. Can we hope to understand modern Ireland, Finland, Poland, and Israel—to select telling examples—without recognising and evaluating the close attachment of their nations to historic home-lands? In short, history and geography together help substantially to mould the attitudes and policies of nations, even though these may be subject too to sudden and unpredictable changes. Thus since there is history as well as geography behind international politics, the political geographer needs to understand the relevant history if he is to intrude effectively into this study.

While it is clear that independent states emerge on the world stage as the products of history and may be said to have grown by stages, it is important to avoid the not uncommon modern practice of regarding them as organisms and of personifying them—convenient though this latter practice is as a means of shorthand. Certainly there is a fundamental philosophical difference of view as to the importance of the individual within the state community, notably as between, for example, the Anglo-Saxon and Russo-Chinese worlds. But states are comprised only of individuals organised as communities, the decisions and actions of which are necessarily taken by individuals, those in whose hands the duty and power of government lie. Since each state is a unique entity, with characteristics of its own, it is helpful to try to discover what has been called its ' state-idea ' or *raison d'être*. This concept, which goes back to Friedrich Ratzel who pioneered in the field of political geography, refers to the idea for which a state exists, as comprehended by its citizens, and as symbolising their loyalty. Clearly the degree to which the state-idea is grasped and accepted by the citizens of a state provides a useful index of its social cohesion and political unity. The interest and value of this concept may be admitted, yet in the search for it in a particular case it is easier to travel hopefully than to arrive. It would also appear easier, by a process of analysis and/or confident guesswork, to determine the state-idea of countries other than one's own. We might usefully discuss in 1965 what is the state-idea of the United Kingdom at what is clearly a critical juncture in its history. Did world-wide ' empire ' explain its *raison d'être* in the days before the British Empire was liquidated ? Did association with the six members of the Common Market appear in 1965 to offer the United Kingdom a new European rôle and purpose ? Or does its state-idea today, as in the last three centuries, reside essentially in its world-wide interests, exemplified by its senior membership and leadership of the Commonwealth and its necessity to trade anywhere and everywhere ? On the other hand, we might with more confidence seek to test the hypotheses that Switzerland's *raison d'être* lies in its attachment to neutrality, that Israel's is related to the ancient association of the Jews with Palestine—the Holy Land, and that the

U.S.S.R.'s is the application of an ideology of a dogmatic yet increasingly elastic kind, designed and intended for the whole world.

But whatever their reasons for existence and regardless of how well these are understood by their citizens, independent states have notably increased in this century, and most markedly since, and as a result of, the two world wars. Just when the means of communication and transport have brought distant places relatively close and made practicable as never before the efficient administration of ever larger areas, the world has become more broken up and compartmented into independent states which are regarded as separate units in international law. These now number more than twice as many as in 1914 and have become characteristic the world over, not only of Europe, to which they were formerly largely confined.

The number of independent states by continents in 1914 and in 1962

	Europe*	N. America**	S. America	M. America***	Asia	Africa	Australasia	
1914	23	1	10	9	6	2	0	51
1962	33	3	10	13	28	28	2	117

* including the U.S.S.R., Turkey, Cyprus, and four microstates which are sovereign in status, but not counting divided Berlin
** taken to include Cuba
*** including Mexico

Note: States subject to protectorate status or without control of their own foreign affairs have not been enumerated above.

The sharp changes in the political map are most evident in Africa and in Asia—the one largely a continent of primitive cultures penetrated by Europeans only during the last hundred years, the other, in contrast, anciently the home of civilisations yet for long largely submissive to external—European and American—imperial control.

The reasons for these latter-day trends towards political independence are broadly familiar. The two world wars which began in Europe brought about the collapse of large, multinational, imperial structures in response to new and strong revolutionary claims for national ' self-determination.' [1] Either during or at the end of World War I the Austro-Hungarian, German, Turkish, and Russian empires

[1] C. E. Carrington, *The Liquidation of the British Empire* (1961), pp. 21–5.

broke up to give rise to so-called successor 'nation states,' although most of the Russian Empire emerged in modern dress as the Union of Soviet Socialist Republics. The British, French, Dutch, and Belgian empires weathered World War I only to dissolve during or after World War II. 'Decolonisation' has become the order of the day, so that the 'colony' or dependent state becomes increasingly rare as newly independent ones, often of doubtful political strength, become more numerous. Membership of the United Nations Organisation, which numbered 51 at its inception in 1945, had grown to 105 by 1962 —and little colonialism remains as a target for nationalistic efforts.

But whereas political power was formerly spread among a number of 'great powers,' so-called, most of which lay in Europe, it is now largely shared by two sub-continental giants, the one lying wholly outside Europe, the other only partly within it. The now immeasurably superior military and economic strength of the U.S.A. and the U.S.S.R., which vie with each other for world leadership, clearly dwarfs the power and ability of other states either to exercise world power or indeed to go it alone. Thus the multi-national Commonwealth, which has succeeded the politically powerful British Empire, survives as a loosely organised world entity only by the good will of the United States, which, through the North Atlantic Treaty Organisation and the ANZUS Pact above all, shares responsibility for its defence. Similarly, notwithstanding President de Gaulle's illusions of greatness, France and the French Community function only behind the NATO shield. As to the many other independent states of lesser political status, attention turns to the concept of political viability : by what means can they hope to achieve their purposes and at the same time preserve their independence from strong external and, in some cases too, internal pressures ? The inter-war years showed, notably in Europe, the weakness and dependence of the new allegedly 'nation' states. Some of them, made up of territories detached from former large working units, often fell far short of national homogeneity. Indeed some, like Yugoslavia, Czechoslovakia, and Poland, contained sizeable national minority groups which proved sources of weakness. The policy too of setting up tariff barriers against neighbouring countries sharpened political division and hindered economic progress. Most of the newly emerged states, notably in Africa,[1]

---

[1] Thus a geographical expert on Africa, Dr G. H. T. Kimble, is reported as believing that not more than 6 of the 26 newly independent African states have

enclosed within arbitrary boundaries originally chosen by their imperial rulers and poorly supported by underdeveloped economies, face dubious prospects of successfully charting their courses alone in the troubled seas of international politics.

Thus, while nation states offer desirable conditions for cultural self-expression and represent genuine political ideals, they have come increasingly to appear parochial and inadequate in a world which commands, as never before, the scientific and technological power to develop Man's estate and material well-being. Their boundaries appear rigid and limiting as frameworks for modern living, and the notion of ' independence' intrudes unhelpfully in an interdependent world. More and more therefore it now seems necessary for states to associate together for common purposes, in varying degrees defensive, cultural, economic, and political. We are witnessing the early stages of attempts to create regional organisations at a higher level, groupings of states willing to act in concert for specific purposes which are nowadays commonly referred to as ' blocs ' (Fig. 73). The present political situation of the world is thus paradoxical : in the heyday of the independent state, with all its separative tendencies, the movement gathers strength for the formation of large multi-national units. And in so far as these seek to function effectively, this involves some abandonment of those sovereign powers which are the prize and hallmark of the independent state.

The word ' bloc,' so familiar today, deserves brief consideration. So spelt, it does not appear in Dr Johnson's dictionary, nor indeed in the *Oxford Shorter English Dictionary* of 1933, although it finds a place in the Supplement to the large *A New English Dictionary* published at Oxford the same year. Webster's *New International Dictionary*, 1937 edition, gives three senses in which this word is currently used. The third of these is particularly well expressed : ' a combination of persons, or interests, usually inharmonious, but temporarily drawn together in a common cause.' In international politics, therefore, this word, which appears to be something of a novelty and to derive from French, has a wide application to denote any combination of states made to foster particular interests and purposes. Webster's use of the words ' inharmonious ' and ' temporarily ' is worth noting for its

a chance of surviving as ' truly autonomous, virile, and stable members of the family of nations.' American Geographical Society Newsletter, winter 1962–3, p. 2.

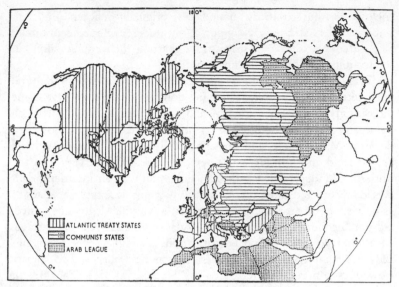

FIG. 73   Some international blocs : NATO, the Communist realm, and the Arab League.

acuteness and relevance to the international blocs with which we are here concerned.

The creation of blocs is not in itself a novel thing, since international differences and conflicts have been continual in modern history and few states have felt strong or safe enough to stand alone. Few have been able to avoid joining alliances with others as have Switzerland on the basis of its armed neutrality and the United States during its long period of isolationism. Commonly many nationalities were grouped within imperial states, held together under the power, coercive at times, of the imperial government. So also states entered freely into defensive alliances, seeking collective security. The blocs of today show both similarities and differences when compared with those of the past. As in the past, they may take the form of alliances freely entered into or, in the Communist world, they may involve an element of coercion as was characteristic of the old empires. On the other hand, they are now different in that they seek to achieve closer and more variously functional unity, having been made, usually on a regional basis, not only for defence but also for political, economic, and cultural purposes. The fashionable and loosely used word ' integration ' typifies the current trend in attitudes and policies, but it is necessary to discover in what respects unity is sought. Clearly a bloc may be formed to promote certain loosely defined cultural and political purposes, as in the case of the Arab League, or specific economic ends, as in that of the European Coal and Steel Community.

The existence of blocs is an evident reflection of the fact that the creation of a world community under one government cannot presently be achieved ; it also soberly recognises the failure of the United Nations Organisation to attain this high ideal. The present-day use of the word 'community' indicates much higher aspirations than in the past. Indeed, it strikes a revolutionary note in that it throws down a challenge to traditional and outworn concepts of nationalism and state sovereignty. Some of the regional blocs of today envisage, or are actively moving towards, the objective of a supra-national state. In so far as this is so, through the creation of effectively functioning political blocs, mankind may be moving haltingly towards the ultimate ideal of unification in one fraternal world such as Buddhism, Christianity, and Islam tried but failed to attain.[1]

Let us look briefly at some of the many international blocs, with an eye on their membership, purposes, degree of cohesion, political status, and prospects. The United Nations Organisation stands out on ground of its approach to universality—in respect of independent states. It provides a forum for political discussion in its General Assembly, where each member has an equal voice, but pays respect to the gross inequality in the distribution of political power in its Security Council, where five states hold permanent seats.[2] Containing as it does many blocs, such as the Arab and Afro-Asian blocs, it exposes, as it gives vent to, the many political differences which divide the world and underlines the present impracticability of world unity. A great deal of the work of UNO is basic and valuable, being conducted by its Agencies, set up to deal with specific, technical matters, such as health, and food and agriculture. That it provides the machinery for dealing with international problems which threaten the peace is clearly important. That it has the ability to use force to this end has been shown by its rôle in the Korean war [3] and its intervention in the former

---

[1] Cf. Maximilien Sorre, *L'Homme sur la Terre* (1961), p. 239.

[2] Anomalously, one of these five is occupied by Formosa, not by the Chinese People's Republic.

[3] UNO's ability to organise military resistance to the invasion of South Korea in 1953 was only made possible because of the temporary withdrawal of the U.S.S.R. member from the Security Council.

Belgian Congo and in Cyprus. Here then is a bloc made up of inharmonious elements, though not a temporary one, it is to be hoped, and one which may, at best and in the long run, as national attitudes and understanding change, point the way to a united world.

The Commonwealth, as a unique institution associating together in friendly co-operation nearly a quarter of mankind [1] distributed in all the continents, is the next important bloc on ground of its scale and world-wide range. Its strength lies in the fact that its members have freely chosen to stay together and that English speech, institutions, law, and liberal thought are in large measure shared. It has practical utility too through the functioning of the sterling area and through its organisation for the day-to-day exchange of information and for periodical discussions of common interests. It is not unimportant also that it implies friendly relations between members and mutual support ; the latter is illustrated by the help which was promptly offered by the United Kingdom to India when in danger from Chinese attack. In so far as it has common objectives in international politics, these might seem to lie in the pursuit of peace, freedom, and the rule of law. In terms of political and military power, however, the Commonwealth does not constitute a bloc. Certainly it cannot be reckoned a ' great power,' for it has no common foreign and defence policies ; nor do any of its members command in scale those expensive nuclear weapons now thought necessary to deter a major assault. The United Kingdom, having lost an empire, finds itself no more than the senior partner in the Commonwealth, and, while it is bound by certain specific defence commitments, as for example to the Malay Federation, it has no longer either the means or the obligation to shoulder the imperial defence burden that lay heavily upon it early in this century. Actually, by the ANZUS Pact, the defence of Australia and New Zealand devolves largely on the U.S.A., while the United Kingdom and Canada, as members of NATO, fall within this defence organisation in which the U.S.A. has preponderant strength.

The Commonwealth, united formally and symbolically only by its Head, who is also Queen of the United Kingdom, Canada, Australia, and New Zealand, is, to repeat, loosely organised and in no sense a super-state. Some have regretted that it failed to expand to include

---

[1] Whereas the population of the Commonwealth exceeds 700 millions, that of remaining dependent territories of the United Kingdom has shrunk to less than 40 millions.

Moslem countries of the Middle East formerly mandated to the United Kingdom, and also some of the smaller countries of Europe, such as Belgium and the Netherlands. Certainly the Commonwealth is not without internal disharmonies at times, witness the prolonged Indo-Pakistan dispute over Kashmir. It continues to increase in membership, but whether or not it will last and even grow in cohesion and political effectiveness raises fit problems for discussion.

Other notable blocs are regional in character though varied in scale. The greatest of these is the Organisation of American States. This is a vast regional confederation, with membership open to all the independent republics of the Americas, although Cuba was recently excluded on a majority vote. It functions effectively by means of an Inter-American Conference, a Council, and a Secretariat—the Pan-American Union. It emerged only in 1948 but marks the culmination of United States policy, persistent though changeful, with reference to the countries of the western hemisphere. This success in associating closely for collective security and peaceful collaboration the peoples of two continents—which however contain scarcely one-seventh of the world's population—had its roots long ago in the Monroe Doctrine which grew out of President Monroe's message to Congress in 1823. In the light of this doctrine the United States has eventually succeeded in creating a bloc of republican states safe from the political intrusion of European powers. The continental unity of the pattern of O.A.S. is impaired only by the fact that Canada, Cuba, and a number of small dependent states are not members. That O.A.S. has a certain strength and solidarity is shown by the way in which its members backed United States policy with respect to the U.S.S.R. over Cuba in 1962. That it encounters serious difficulties, chiefly because the U.S.A. has overwhelming superiority and regards the Caribbean world as its frontier, has been specially evident again since the San Domingo uprising of 1965.

Nearer at home, in our own continent, bloc formation, both west and east of the Iron Curtain, has been vigorous since the end of the Second World War. Several distinct reasons explain these remarkable developments. In western Europe fear of further Soviet expansion underlined the need for the collective organisation of defence under the leadership of the United States : hence the NATO alliance of 1949 which induced the U.S.S.R.'s counterpoise, the Warsaw Pact Organisation of 1955. Another reason sprang from the growing interdependence of modern industry and the advantages of closer economic co-operation. This accounts for the Organisation for European Co-operation and Development, which now includes nineteen European countries west of the Iron Curtain. For similar reasons, namely the economies to be made in larger areas of production and trade, six countries agreed to form the European Coal and Steel Community in 1952 and to operate under a supra-national High Authority. In 1958 the same six launched the European Economic Community (the

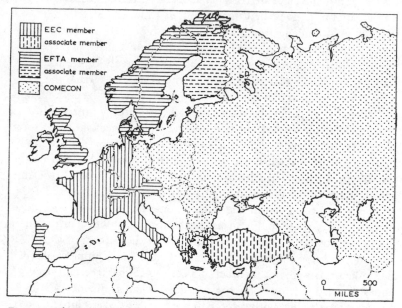

Fig. 74   The patterns of the European Economic Community, the European Free Trade Association, and the Council for Mutual Economic Assistance.

Note that Greece and Turkey are ' associate ' members of EEC and that Finland is an associate member of EFTA.

Common Market, so-called) and also the European Atomic Community to develop the peaceful uses of atomic energy. In reaction to E.E.C. and under British leadership, the European Free Trade Association (the Outer Seven so-called) was formed in 1960 by seven other members of O.E.C.D. (Fig. 74). In Communist Europe the Council for Mutual Economic Assistance (C.M.E.A. or COMECON) was set up by the European satellites of the U.S.S.R. in 1949 and more recently this has been used in the attempt to co-ordinate their economic plans. The more recent attempts, organised originally by Khrushchev, have faced strong nationalistic opposition, notably in Rumania, and have in some measure failed.

E.E.C. is of special interest, for it would seem to mark a turning point in history and a movement away from the narrow nationalisms which have so long and so restrictively flourished. Its conception combines a clear regard to the material interests of its members with an imaginative belief in the virtues of close international collaboration. E.E.C. is, on the one hand, a well organised economic bloc which is steadily realising its agreed aims, and on the other, potentially a new multi-national state of the future. In this respect E.E.C. recalls, as it may come to illustrate, Lord Acton's view that 'Those States are substantially the most perfect which . . . include distinct nationalities without oppressing them.' . . . 'The combination of different nations in one State is as necessary a condition of civilised life as the combination of man in society.' [1]

By the Treaty of Rome, France, the Federal German Republic, Italy, and the three Benelux countries agreed to work together to create, after a transitional period of 12–15 years, a common market within a common external tariff system. Quotas on trade between the Six have already been abolished ; internal tariffs have been much reduced and should disappear by 1967, while their unequal external tariffs are being, and will continue to be, steadily aligned to common levels. The bloc uses the Assembly and the Court of Justice which had already been created for the European Coal and Steel Community. It has also a Council of Ministers (six in number) and a Commission of nine members. These bodies devise policy for the Community as a whole, while the Commission has also an executive rôle. Measures are being taken by stages to co-ordinate the agriculture of the Six and to protect it by levies imposed on imports from external producers ; also to ease, and eventually to free, the movement of capital and labour. A remarkable historical aspect of E.E.C. is that Franco-German co-operation replaces Franco-German hostility. It has clearly acquired a high degree of internal cohesion and the ability to withstand such strains as Britain's application for entry imposed upon it. That it has also proved successful economically is shown by the 29 per cent increase in industrial production which it achieved during its first four years, 1958–61. Its economic stature is evident from the fact that it

[1] Lord Acton, ' Essay on Nationality ' (1862), in *The History of Freedom and other Essays* (1919), pp. 298 and 290.

has become the greatest trading unit in the world. And it is already in some measure a supra-national entity : the diplomatic representatives of 34 countries are accredited to it.

The Treaty of Rome is in many ways a remarkable document. It is enough to note here some of its original provisions. First, it created institutions with clearly specified powers and functions. In particular, the Commission was so conceived as to provide a strong and efficient executive body. Its membership includes not more than two nationals of any one of the six states who have to be chosen on grounds of their personal competence and independence of mind. Second, the Treaty laid down clearly and almost rigidly the programme of action to be taken during the transitional period, as also procedures on voting in the Assembly, Council, and Commission. Third, it opened up much wider prospects than a Community only of the Six. Article 110 stated that the member states would try to contribute, in the common interest, to the harmonious development of world trade ; Article 237 that any European state could apply for membership, and Article 131 that non-European countries and territories, in special relations with Belgium, France, Italy, and the Netherlands, would be associated with the Community.

E.E.C. was conceived as a move towards the unification of western Europe. The United States supported this venture, scarcely helpful though it has been to its own export trade, on the political and defence grounds that it would strengthen its European partners in NATO. For the same reasons it urged the United Kingdom to seek entry. Actually E.E.C. has grown only by the admission, as associated members, of Greece, Turkey and eighteen non-European countries, mainly in Africa, which stood in special relations to one of the Six. The United Kingdom was unprepared to join the Common Market as a founding member in 1958, being mindful of its trade commitments to Commonwealth countries and unready also to envisage yielding up a measure of its sovereignty. Instead it organised a group of European trade partners, who were willing to make mutual reductions of tariffs on manufactured goods, as the European Free Trade Association. This consists, in addition to the United Kingdom, of Austria, Denmark, Switzerland, Norway, Sweden, Portugal, together with Finland as an associate member.

The failure of Britain's application to join the Common Market, after long and arduous negotiations, because of the opposition of France, hardly favours the application of a number of other interested countries. Denmark, Norway and Ireland seek full membership; Austria, Portugal, Spain, Sweden, Switzerland, and Cyprus associate membership. As a move towards European economic integration therefore, E.E.C. has been dubiously successful. While it has certainly promoted close economic collaboration by the Six as a foundation upon which their political union may ultimately be built, it has created further disunity in Europe. Of the nineteen members of the Organization for European Co-operation and Development, eight were (in the spring of 1964) grouped in the Common Market, eight, including the United Kingdom, were members of the European Free Trade Association, and the remaining three—Ireland, Iceland, and Spain—lie outside both groups. In short, doubts and problems arise as to the path which E.E.C. may now be following and whether this will lead towards the high ideals of an expanding community such as the Treaty of Rome appeared to envisage. Certainly the Six themselves are already contemplating the political union for which their close economic co-operation is preparing them. Already in July 1961 the governments of the Six requested the formulation of a draft treaty of union, and although differences arose as to the form this should take, one can only be impressed by this revolutionary prospect which draws support from big business and trade unions alike. Yet those left outside E.E.C., and some of those included in it, may wonder whether, in so far as President de Gaulle is able to achieve his ends, the Common Market is destined to become for a time an 'isolationist power-bloc of the rich' rather than a means to wider unification such as would embody present-day aspirations.

Western Europe thus remains politically divided but the creation of a multi-national state, made up of the Six, seems likely, if not imminent. With the United Kingdom and other would-be members added, E.E.C. could become a political unit of high stature, in population numbers and economic resources comparable with, or indeed greater than, either the United States or the Soviet Union. On 4 July 1962, in a speech at Philadelphia, President Kennedy offered to such an expanded E.E.C. partnership, as an equal, with the United States. Such an Atlantic Community, if politically integrated, would surely control the greatest economic and military resources in the world. But President de Gaulle, in reaction to America's leadership as also to the Anglo-Saxon Atlantic world, envisages E.E.C. in continental terms as a third force. Under French leadership, it might praise, in his view, to the rôle of unifier of Europe, east and west alike.

Yet, in so far as these ideas have long-term practical value, it must be remembered that western Europe is not militarily a third force but depends for its security on the NATO shield which derives its strength from the deterrent weapons of the United States. It seemed for a time, as it may well appear later on, that Britain, having lost an empire, might find a new rôle for which it seemed well cast, by providing the needed bridge between the North Atlantic and west European members of a great multi-national partnership based on broad cultural affinities.

In eastern Europe, too, political, economic, and military collaboration has made marked advances. The U.S.S.R.'s military power since the last years of World War II has made possible the projection of Soviet ideology and the establishment of totalitarian régimes in four states beyond its European border, as also in Eastern Germany, Bulgaria, and Albania. Thus the U.S.S.R. has been able to create, east of the Iron Curtain, another bloc of states. Standing uneasily apart from the western and eastern defensive blocs, organised by NATO and the Warsaw Pact, are a number of neutral or neutralist states—Ireland, Switzerland, Austria, Sweden, and Yugoslavia. In addition, Spain and Finland are not formally aligned, although the former provides aero-naval bases for the United States, and the latter, under the shadow of its mighty neighbour, enjoys little freedom of action in foreign affairs.

Gone are the days when world power could be sustained from so small a territorial base as the British Isles. The principal actors in the struggle for world leadership now occupy territories of continental or, more strictly, sub-continental scale. The Communist bloc, embracing 36 per cent of mankind, has the more continental aspect, in that, apart from its Cuban outlier, it extends from the U.S.S.R.'s European borderlands to the Arctic and the Pacific, although account should be taken of outlying Communist parties as in Italy and France. In contrast, the western bloc, led from its continental North American base, is widely distributed across the Atlantic and Pacific oceans. It is characteristic of both of these ideologically opposed blocs, which vie with each other to win the support of the neutralist world, that they are far from monolithic. The rift between Mao Tse-Tung and Mr Khrushchev and his successors is balanced by that between Presidents Johnson and de Gaulle. Yet, ironically enough, the two conflicting conceptions of the destiny of mankind rest upon the same belief in the great promise of human betterment offered by modern scientific and technological progress.

Reading List

THE first task of a geographer is the reading of maps, and the use of an atlas or atlases in the study of the relations between geography and history is indispensable.   Above all, the student will find a general physical atlas, such as Philip's *The University Atlas* or Bartholomew's *Advanced Atlas* of great help ; an historical atlas, too, should be consulted.

CHAPTER I

Geography as an Historical Document

There are few works in English on the relations between geography and history.   A pioneer study is *The Relations of Geography and History*, by H. B. George (1st ed., 1901 ; 5th ed., 1924).   *A Geographical Introduction to History* (1925), by L. Febvre, is a stimulating if super-critical review of its subject.   The reader will find many illustrations of the operation of geographical factors in European history if he refers to *An Historical Geography of Europe* (1935), by W. G. East.   Certain aspects of the history of England also are examined geographically in *An Historical Geography of England before 1800* (1936), edited by H. C. Darby, and *The Making of the English Landscape* (1955), by W. G. Hoskins.   On Wales, see E. G. Bowen, *Wales : A Study in Geography and History* (1941) and *The Settlements of the Celtic Saints in Wales* (1954).

CHAPTER II

Old Maps as Historical Documents

For a short competent introduction see G. R. Crone, *Maps and their Makers* (1953), which gives many references to the literature on the history of cartography ;   Sir C. F. Close, *The Map of England* (1932).

CHAPTER III

Geographical Position

This topic usually finds a place in geographical studies of particular countries. For the classic account of the position of Britain see Sir H. J. Mackinder's *Britain and the British Seas* (1902), chapter 1.

CHAPTER IV

Climate and History

The reader may be referred to two works of C. E. P. Brooks, the chief English contributor in this field : *The Evolution of Climate* (1922) and *Climate through the Ages* (1928). The subject of past climates and their relation to history forms the theme of many works by Ellsworth Huntington, to which references are given in *Climatic Changes* (1932), by E. Huntington and S. S. Visher ; see also *Climate and the Energy of Nations* (1942), by S. F. Markham.

CHAPTER V

Routes

On the old roads of England the reader will find much help in H. J. Randall's *History in the Open Air* (1936), chapter II, which includes a short bibliography. A small booklet, priced at sixpence, was issued by H.M. Stationery Office in 1932 : *Field Archæology*. It is a useful guide for a beginner who wishes to understand some of the many evidences of prehistory which are visible in the countryside. Three historical maps, issued by the Ordnance Survey, show former road systems : *Map of Roman Britain* (3rd ed., 1955, with notes), *Seventeenth-Century England and Wales* (1930) ; and a facsimile of the Gough map, which is discussed in the article by F. M. Stenton, cited at the foot of page 64, above. Finally, much information on the past communications of England, together with maps, can be found in H. C. Darby, *op. cit.*

CHAPTER VI

Towns

Studies of particular towns have to be sought in many learned journals. On the origin of towns the reader may turn to V. Gordon Childe's *Man Makes Himself* (1936). For a short survey of towns in their many aspects, see D. V. Glass's *The Town* (1935). Niles Carpenter's *The Sociology of City Life* (1931) discusses many matters of geographical and historical interest. There is a short account of the origin of European towns in W. G. East, *op. cit.*, especially in chapter VI.

CHAPTER VII

Frontiers and Boundaries

For short general discussions of political frontiers and boundaries see Lord Curzon's *Frontiers* (1907), and C. B. Fawcett's *Frontiers* (1918, out of print). F. de Lapradelle's *La Frontière* (1928), though mainly concerned with the legal aspect, has much to say of geographical and historical interest, and gives numerous references to other works. On the Welsh and Scottish Borders see respectively W. Rees's *South Wales and the March, 1284–1415* (1924), and D. L. W. Tough's *The Last Years of a Frontier : a History of the Border during the Reign of Elizabeth* (1928). A recent introductory study is J. R. V. Prescott, *The Geography of Frontiers and Boundaries* (1965).

CHAPTER VIII

Habitat and Economy

For general discussions of the relationship between economic activities and the physical environment see P. Vidal de la Blache's *Principles of Human Geography* (1926) ; J. Brunhes's *Human Geography* (1920) ; and L. Febvre, *op. cit.* For particular historical illustrations see C. D. Forde's *Habitat, Economy and Society* (1934) ; W. G. East, *op. cit.* ; and H. C. Darby, *op. cit.*

CHAPTER IX

The Dawn of Civilisation

The works of V. Gordon Childe give clear and authoritative expositions of the beginnings of civilisation. See his *More Light on the Most Ancient East* (1933), *The Dawn of European Civilization* (1925), and *Man Makes Himself* (1936). For a general discussion of the origin of civilisations see A. J. Toynbee's *A Study of History*, vol. ii (2nd ed., 1935). J. L. Myres's *The Dawn of History* (1911) gives due weight to the geographical factor in the rise of ancient civilisations and states. H. J. E. Peake and H. J. Fleure in *The Corridors of Time* summarise, on a chronological basis and in relation to the geographical background, the succession of early cultures.

CHAPTER X

The Dawn of Civilisation in the Americas

The annotation to books and articles in periodicals given in this chapter indicates the range of literature on matters which will necessarily continue to remain under discussion.

CHAPTER XI

Europe and China

On this broad topic the following works serve as an introduction: G. F. Hudson's *Europe and China : A Survey of their Relations from the Earliest Times to 1800* (1931) ; E. E. Power's 'The Opening of the Land Routes to Cathay' (during the period 1245–1345), in *Travel and Travellers of the Middle Ages* (1930), edited by A. P. Newton ; E. H. Warmington's *The Commerce between the Roman Empire and India* (1928) ; and C. N. Parkinson's *Trade in the Eastern Seas, 1793–1813* (1937). Many valuable papers on the historical geography of China by P. M. Roxby have been published in *Geography*.

A valuable atlas, by A. Herrmann, is the *Historical and Commercial Atlas of China* (Harvard University Press, 1935). A competent account of travel through Central Asia is Sir E. Teichman's *Journey to Turkestan* (1937). Marco Polo's *Travels* was issued in a convenient edition in the Travellers' Library in 1928.

CHAPTER XII

International Politics

Among geographical studies in this field note *The Changing World* (1956), edited by W. G. East and A. E. Moodie ; *The Changing Map of Asia* (4th ed., 1961), edited by W. G. East and O. H. K. Spate. Van Nostrand's 'Searchlight Books' discuss a wide range of political problems in specific areas. For reference the following introductory study is of value, *Foundations of International Politics* (Van Nostrand, 1962), by H. and M. Sprout.

Index